AN EXECUTIVE GUIDE TO IFRS

AN EXECUTIVE GUIDE TO IFRS

CONTENT, COSTS AND BENEFITS TO BUSINESS

PETER WALTON

WILEY

A John Wiley and Sons, Ltd, Publication

This edition first published 2011
© 2011 John Wiley & Sons, Ltd

Registered office
John Wiley & Sons Ltd, The Atrium, Southern Gate, Chichester, West Sussex, PO19 8SQ, United Kingdom

For details of our global editorial offices, for customer services and for information about how to apply for permission to reuse the copyright material in this book please see our website at www.wiley.com.

Library of Congress Cataloging-in-Publication Data
Walton, Peter J.
  An executive guide to IFRS : content, costs and benefits to business / Peter Walton.
    p. cm.
  Includes bibliographical references and index.
  ISBN 978-0-470-66490-2 (pbk.)
1. Financial statements—Standards. 2. International business enterprises—Accounting—Standards. 3. International financial reporting standards. I. Title.
  HF5626W35 2011
  657'.30218—dc22   2011007568

A catalogue record for this book is available from the British Library.

ISBN 978-0-470-66490-2 (paperback), ISBN 978-1-119-97447-5 (ebk),
ISBN 978-1-119-97385-0 (ebk), ISBN 978-1-119-97386-7 (ebk)

Typeset in 10/12pt Adobe Garamond Pro by Sparks – www.sparkspublishing.com
Printed and bound in Great Britain byTJ International Ltd, Padstow, Cornwall, UK

CONTENTS

PREFACE

This book is intended to be an easily accessible guide to the particularities of International Financial Reporting Standards (IFRS). The reader I had in mind is the accountant, the analyst, the financial executive or indeed the student of accounting, who is familiar with one or other form of national Generally Accepted Accounting Principles (GAAP) and wishes to familiarize themselves with IFRS for whatever reason. The book will not therefore teach you basic accounting nor tell you how to prepare financial statements under IFRS, but it will present as clearly as possible the main particularities that you should be aware of.

My initial training was in UK GAAP but I have since worked with US GAAP, French GAAP and Swiss GAAP as well as IFRS, and the choice of issues to highlight is informed by that background. I have spent many, many days listening to the IASB at work as an observer in the public gallery since April 2001, and I have tried to bring a flavour of the insights gained from that experience.

I should add the regular disclaimer that books like this are general in nature and are not a substitute for dedicated professional advice. If you would like to contact me, I can be reached at walton@ifrsnews.net. Suggestions for improvements are always welcome.

ACKNOWLEDGEMENTS

I am grateful to Jenny McCall, the commissioning editor, for her interest in the project and her support. I should also like to thank Gemma Valler, Amy Webster and their colleagues at John Wiley & Sons for their input in bringing the book to the market.

I should like to thank the Trustees of the IFRS Foundation for permission to cite extracts from IFRS and related literature. I should also like to express my appreciation of the generally sociable and helpful attitude of IASB members and staff during the many days I have spent observing them at work in the Cannon Street offices and elsewhere.

I should like to thank Steve Collings of Leavitt Walmsley Associates for his helpful comments on the first draft of this book. I am also grateful to Philippe Danjou (IASB) for comments on the last chapter. I, of course, remain responsible for errors.

ABOUT THE AUTHOR

Peter Walton has worked as an accountant with British and French multinationals and been finance director of a listed company. He subsequently moved to journalism, research and teaching. He researched a PhD at the London School of Economics and has taught at universities in the UK, US, Switzerland and France. He is chairman of the European Accounting Association's Financial Reporting Standards Committee, which coordinates the EAA's inputs to IFRS.

Peter is currently a Professor of Accounting at ESSEC Business School, Paris, where he is IFRS Director of the ESSEC-KPMG Financial Reporting Centre. He edits *IFRS Monitor*, a monthly report of the proceedings of the IASB, which is used by auditing firms, standard-setters and companies (www.ifrsmonitor.com). He also edits *World Accounting Report*, a monthly bulletin on international financial reporting.

CHAPTER 1

WORLDWIDE CONVERGENCE ON IFRS

This chapter is introductory in nature. It explains the origins of the use of IFRS for multinational companies and the notion of convergence. It reviews the progress of convergence and the case for and against use of a single comprehensive basis of accounting in the international capital markets.

In this century, financial reporting by large companies has undergone a transformation. In 2000 there was a picture of global diversity with each multinational mostly using the accounting rules of the country where it maintained its head office and (usually) primary stock exchange listing, with US principles dominant where a choice was available. By 2010 the world had changed to one where many of the top international companies use international rules: International Financial Reporting Standards, or IFRS.

The main aim of this book is to introduce to you the principal features of IFRS and provide some of the context to help explain the role of IFRS in the world. It will also tell you how IFRS are formulated and how you can influence that process and be part of it if you wish. The first chapter looks at the convergence process and tells you the story so far. The following section is the main technical content of the book – an analysis of the main issues under IFRS reporting. This includes a chapter devoted to the *IFRS for SMES*. The final section tells you about how IFRS are created and gives you some of the historical background, as well as some comments on the fundamental thinking behind IFRS.

Although IFRS have been developing since as far back as 1973, their role in international capital markets started when the International Organization of Securities Commissions (IOSCO) decided in the 1980s to develop an international 'passport' for companies seeking secondary listings on foreign stock exchanges. At that time each major stock exchange had its own listing requirements – the information that it asked companies to provide if they wanted their securities quoted on the exchange. The requirements were less for secondary listings (i.e. companies whose home exchange was elsewhere) but nonetheless were different country by country. In particular, a company could find itself having to produce accounting information on several different bases, which was very costly.

IOSCO, which is a voluntary association of national stock exchange regulators such as the SEC (Securities and Exchange Commission), decided that it should organize a uniform approach to secondary listings. The idea was that if a company provided information – financial statements and other disclosures – in a uniform manner, this information package would be accepted for secondary listings anywhere in the world. This would significantly cut the cost of listing and provide more encouragement to companies to seek new markets.

IOSCO got together with the international accounting standard-setter to work on extending the reach of IFRS (they were then called International Accounting Standards – IAS) to meet this purpose. At the time, the biggest incentive was access to the US capital market.

The SEC required foreign companies to either provide full US GAAP[1] financial statements or supply domestic statements with a reconciliation of earnings and net assets to what they would have been under US GAAP, known as the '20F reconciliation' after the SEC form. People hoped that a successful IOSCO passport would enable them to prepare IFRS statements without a reconciliation.

Convergence

This would have led to widespread use of IAS/IFRS for secondary listings. In addition, some countries already used them either to meet gaps in local rules or as the model for national rules. However, everything changed in 2000 when the convergence initiative could be said to have taken over. In 1999 the international standard-setter completed an overhaul of its standards and in May 2000 IOSCO accepted them as the basis of its secondary listing approach. But in June the European Commission announced that it would bring forward legislation to make IAS/IFRS compulsory for the **primary** financial statements of companies listed on European Union (EU) stock exchanges. This was the start of the worldwide move to use only IAS/IFRS for financial statements provided by companies using public capital markets. National GAAP was set to disappear progressively and be replaced by IAS/IFRS, at first in the EU but progressively in Australia, South Africa, Canada, India, Brazil, South Korea, Japan, China and many other countries. Even the US is thinking about it.

Convergence, then, is the move towards using a single, globally accepted set of financial reporting standards in preference to using standards developed nationally. Why has the world suddenly decided after centuries of national rules that international ones are necessary? The short answer is that the world economy is increasingly being

---

1 Generally Accepted Accounting Principles – an expression that is used to designate the totality of standards, rules, etc., that govern financial statements in any country.

polarized into small and large business, and financial reporting is also being polarized as it responds to business needs.

Smaller businesses do not typically have foreign subsidiaries nor do they raise finance on the public markets. Their financial statements are used primarily for tax assessment and to provide confirmation to bank lenders of the information given in management accounts and estimates. The main influence on their rules is likely to be national taxation.

Listed companies, on the other hand, need to communicate with a wide range of external stakeholders, especially the capital markets. They have to compete with other companies for finance and it is in their interests for their financial statements to be comparable. A market investor will ask for a higher return to compensate for higher risk. Lack of knowledge of the basis of accounting used is regarded as a risk factor and will therefore cause shares to be more expensive for the issuer. IAS/IFRS are now widely understood and accepted, not only in markets where they are the required reporting base. Consequently a foreign company using IAS/IFRS is able to present itself in a manner that does not increase perceived risk – raising capital in the public markets is cheaper under IAS/IFRS!

Lack of knowledge of the basis of accounting is regarded as a risk factor and will therefore cause shares to be more expensive for the issuer

Market pressures have pushed governments to recognize that large companies are different animals, with different accounting needs, from smaller companies, and to accept that different sets of accounting rules can co-exist within the same economy. While it has gone for global convergence on IFRS for listed companies, the EU is planning to give member states the right to exempt companies with fewer than 10 employees from producing any accounts at all. This is a direct reversal of its policies in the 1970s and 1980s when, through a series of company law directives, it sought to establish the same accounting for all companies, even if smaller ones had fewer disclosures.

Large company advantages

Depending on the circumstances of the company, a multinational should benefit from a number of cost savings when using IFRS. As discussed, there should be a reduction in the cost of capital based on the fact that very many investment managers now know and understand the use of IFRS. Consequently the company that wishes to reach a wider group of investors will find IFRS statements accepted in all major markets.

In terms of secondary listings, the use of IFRS will indeed fulfil IOSCO's aim of providing financial statements that stock exchange regulators will accept to support foreign listings. In particular, the SEC in 2007 abandoned the 20F reconciliation for companies that prepared IFRS statements. This means that non-US companies using IFRS can have a New York listing without providing US GAAP information – something that AXA, the French insurer, estimated to cost it in the region of $20m in 2006.

Not all companies want a US or other foreign listing, but some chief financial officers (CFOs) consider that going to a large market enables them to raise capital more cheaply. There is also the argument that a foreign listing also carries with it a lot of publicity in that country and is much cheaper than the equivalent advertising. Bay & Bruns (2003, 386–387) say:

The decision to establish or expand a presence on a foreign capital market allows a company to extend its position as a global financial player as well as to underline its commitment to that foreign market. This signal is strongest when the shares of the company are quoted on the local stock exchange. These apparently rather abstract aims bring with them a number of concrete advantages that support foreign ventures and listings.

Hans-Georg Bruns and Wolf Bay were involved in listing Daimler Benz on the New York Stock Exchange. Dr Bruns was the chief accounting officer when Daimler merged with Chrysler. He was later a member of the International Accounting Standards Board (IASB). Bay & Bruns (2003) suggest that a foreign listing:

- signals that its objective is a long-term involvement in the country
- generates increased interest through financial press analysis and significantly increases a corporation's visibility
- may avoid constraints in its home stock exchange
- enables it to market its financial products to the most appropriate customers.

In principle, reporting using IFRS will make it much cheaper to have secondary listings in other countries, because there is no need for figures drawn up under other accounting bases. It will also result in a better cost of capital because investment managers are increasingly used to IFRS statements.

Moreover, there are other advantages for multinationals. As the number of countries where IFRS are accepted continues to grow, so more and more foreign subsidiaries of multinationals can file local financial statements using IFRS. Traditionally a multinational had two basic choices with foreign subsidiaries: (1) they could install worldwide uniform accounting systems and have all subsidiaries account in the same way, with local GAAP accounts prepared by a local accounting firm; or (2) subsidiaries use local GAAP and their figures are re-stated at head office for consolidation purposes. The use of IFRS as a reporting basis for the group eliminates the need for duplicate sets of numbers.

Peggy Smyth, vice president and controller of United Technologies, the US conglomerate, is a member of the IFRS Interpretations Committee (this provides clarifications – see Chapter 9 for more detail). She told members of the international committee when she was appointed that her company had 60 subsidiaries that used IFRS.

Using IFRS throughout a group has other advantages, such as making the audit easier and also making it easier to move staff around throughout the group without re-training. Preparing internal accounting manuals is more logical and there can be economies in staff training. It is no longer necessary to monitor accounting developments in each of a series of major economies.

Why governments support IFRS

use of IFRS as a reporting basis for the group eliminates the need for duplicate sets of numbers

There are a number of public policy reasons that also support a move to using IFRS. The most fundamental is probably that using the same accounting basis provides greater comparability between companies. Greater comparability in turn should lead to more efficient investment. The argument is (and there is research evidence to support this) that investors are reluctant to invest across national boundaries because they do not understand the financial statements of foreign companies. Investors face therefore a limited choice, which allows inefficient managements to stay in control of assets. Once investors can compare apples with apples, they can invest more efficiently, which in turn should lead to assets being used more productively.

Access to international markets also means that companies can have access to wider sources of finance, which should in turn mean their finance becomes cheaper. Supposing national governments want their domestic businesses to expand, access to foreign financial markets may be important if the domestic financial market is limited. This was one of the reasons cited by the European Commission for moving to IFRS. It would give smaller listed companies access to more liquid markets. In the case of the European Commission there was also the major motive that use of the same accounting basis across the EU would do (and has done) a great deal to create a single European capital market.

Another side of this argument is that helping foreign companies to list in your country makes your domestic financial market busier and gives local investors wider choices. In the past this has been an argument advanced by the New York Stock Exchange to allow companies using IFRS not to have to provide a reconciliation to US GAAP.

The use of IAS/IFRS in the world

In the 1990s, when the international standard-setter was working hard to complete its IOSCO package, its standards were already in use in a number of different ways. A number of European countries allowed domestic multinationals to use IAS if they were active on international capital markets. This was the case for Germany, Belgium and France, within the EU. Italy required the use of IAS by listed companies where national rules had no standard and Switzerland recommended use of IAS. Indeed Swiss international companies such as Nestlé and Roche have long reported using international standards.

The World Bank was (and is) a significant agent in encouraging countries to use international standards

In addition to this use by individual companies, a number of developing and newly industrialized countries, such as South Africa, Singapore and Malaysia, used IAS as a model for their domestic standards. These were generally countries with a history of using Anglo-Saxon accounting as a result of their colonial past. The World Bank was (and is) a significant agent in encouraging countries to use international standards. While at the time the international standard-setter was happy to provide this input, it has now resulted in a situation where a number of countries claim that their domestic standards are in line with IAS/IFRS. However, they do not necessarily adopt all the continuing changes to IFRS, and potentially cause confusion in the international markets by offering slightly different variants.

One of the issues in this situation is that countries are understandably reluctant to give up their freedom to regulate accounting in their own country. By issuing a local variant they retain the notion of local control, but at the cost of potentially not having their standards accepted as being as good as IAS/IFRS, and therefore not gaining the full benefits from the international markets. When Australia first adopted IFRS in 2005, it took the opportunity to remove some options from them, but finally changed its mind. The regulators took the view that being able to say they used full IFRS was more useful.

The French government in particular has most publicly had difficulties in coming to terms with using IFRS. President Jacques Chirac famously wrote to the Commission in 2004 asking them to modify the accounting for financial instruments and assert European authority. In 2009, French finance minister Christine Lagarde similarly wrote demanding that the IASB's financial instrument proposals be stopped. A report to the French parliament in 2009 agreed that IFRS were a reality, but asked the French government to use the European endorsement mechanism to modify IFRS as used in the EU. Such attempts to modify IFRS can also damage the credibility of worldwide convergence. Governments in effect give away some part of everybody's gains in order to try to get a package that suits them.

The EU has, however, been a catalyst in the progress of IFRS. When it announced in 2000 that it would adopt them from 2005, it started a momentum that is still continuing. Australia and South Africa decided to switch at the same time and, at the time of writing, more than 100 countries worldwide either require or permit the use of IFRS for listed companies. 2011 has been fixed by the G20 countries for US GAAP to be converged with IFRS so that there is a single global standard.

It remains a question as to whether US GAAP, which operates in a very litigious and law-oriented environment, can converge in great detail with IFRS that have to be written without reference to a national legal framework. It is, however, true that a number of major economies will be moving very shortly to the use of IFRS. China has mandated since 2007 its own Accounting Standards for Business Enterprises that are modelled on IFRS and are not that distant. Listed companies in Brazil moved in 2010. Canada, Korea and the largest listed companies in India are moving in 2011. Argentina, Mexico and Malaysia are moving in 2012. Japanese companies can adopt voluntarily and the country will decide in 2011 whether to make IFRS compulsory.

The SEC published a road map for discussion in 2008. This would have had an IFRS decision made in 2011, followed by a stepped adoption for US listed companies from 2012. However, since that draft road map was published the US has experienced a change of government and the full effects of the financial crisis. Most people do not expect the US to move very soon.

Problems with convergence

Because there are lots of positives for global business in having global accounting standards, this does not mean that there are not negatives as well. From the individual company perspective, the biggest disadvantage is the cost of making the transition. All the accounting managers in a group will need training, and there may be significant systems changes as well. Estimates of costs vary. A study by the Institute of Chartered Accountants of England and Wales for the European Commission suggested the following estimate:

- companies with turnover below €500m: 0.31% of turnover
- companies with turnover from €500m to €5,000m: 0.05% of turnover
- companies with turnover above €5,000m: 0.05% of turnover.

Clearly the cost varies a lot with size and with the extent to which you can use your own staff to carry out the transition as opposed to hiring outside consultants. It also depends on whether you were already using accounting standards that were similar to IFRS, such as US GAAP or UK GAAP, or relatively different such as French GAAP or German GAAP. Moving to different standards may also affect your monthly management reports so that it changes how managers see the company.

Not all large companies can get benefits after incurring these costs. The large, national player with little foreign activity and no secondary listings will see very little advantage. The costs of complying with IFRS might even persuade some smaller listed companies to de-list. Accounting costs least per transaction for the largest companies, and bears disproportionately on smaller companies.

Another disadvantage for companies is that they need to change the way they work with standard-setters. For large companies it was not that difficult to have informal contacts with national standard-setters and indeed ministries to put across a point of view about changes. Under an IFRS system, national government has much less influence on standard-setting – not least

From the individual company perspective, the biggest disadvantage is the cost of making the transition

because there are many governments using IFRS. Companies need to find different ways to participate in the standard-setting process. (This is quite easily done by sending people to working groups, offering to field test proposed changes, etc., as we will explore in Chapter 9.)

One of the reasons for the rise of IFRS is that governments, and for that matter companies and stock exchanges, are generally quite reluctant to spend any money on formulating accounting standards. Consequently they are in normal times quite happy to use a 'free' import of reputable standards. However, the financial crisis showed that in difficult times governments do not then have control of the standard-setting process. The French government took the view that measuring banks' financial instruments at fair value (current market value) was exacerbating the collapse of the market. It wanted to change the way French banks account but could not do so. It had to build a coalition of EU member states, and threaten action that would have jeopardized global convergence, to get what it wanted. The financial crisis underlined that global convergence also involves loss of sovereignty.

Another question is whether using converged standards gets you converged financial statements. After the 2005 EU adoption of IFRS many studies show that different companies interpret IFRS differently, and commentators question whether convergence achieves anything. Part of this question is whether you thought financial reporting in a country was uniform **before** convergence. Research suggests that it was not, and there is always room for subjective judgement in financial reporting. Therefore it may be that the variability that some people report now has always been there and has nothing to do with IFRS.

At the same time, many efforts have been made to put structures in place to minimize different national interpretations. On a global level the standard-setter has its own interpretations body (the International Financial Reporting Interpretations Committee – IFRIC) that provides detailed rulings. There are often national interpretations bodies that can and do make local rulings. IFRIC tries to liaise with these and ensure consistency. Most countries have stock exchange regulators that carry out scrutiny of company reports. The securities regulators can also therefore make interpretations. Here again efforts are made through regular conferences and also the use of databases of decisions (IOSCO runs one) to ensure that decisions are coherent with each other. Within the EU, regulation of stock exchanges remains national, but there is a coordinating committee (Committee of European Securities Regulators, which became the European Securities and Markets Authority in 2011) that arranges regular exchanges of information between national bodies and also maintains a database of decisions.

The remaining key players are the Big Four international audit firms. Each of them maintains a global IFRS desk in London that liaises with the standard-setter but also tries to ensure consistency of application across their global networks. KPMG doesn't want KPMG Spain approving an application that is prohibited by KPMG Singapore any more than IOSCO wants the Spanish regulator to differ from the Singapore regulators. The auditors have direct oversight of the accounting of their clients and are the front line in maintaining consistency. Another part of this is that they all publish authoritative accounting encyclopaedias that provide a reference for nearly all transactions.

Modified convergence

It is worth pointing out that the literature is starting to refer to convergence in a slightly different sense as well. China, as noted above, has not adopted IFRS as such but has chosen to issue local standards that are largely the same as IFRS but reflect the local economic and legal framework. Japan has said that it will do the same, although it now lets Japanese companies use IFRS voluntarily and may still go for adoption. Convergence in the Chinese manner is therefore slightly different than the general convergence movement discussed above, even though it is a subset of that. Chinese convergence will result in standards very similar to the international model but not the same. A report by the staff of the SEC in October 2010 raised the possibility that this modified convergence might be a route that the US could follow instead of full adoption of IFRS.

Generally the IASB does not like the modified convergence approach. Their call is 'adopt, do not adapt'. It is confusing to investors if there are several comprehensive bases of accounting in use in the international markets, all claiming to be more or less IFRS. Also the IASB does not want its standards devalued (as happened to an extent in the 1990s) by countries using all the standards except the tough ones.

Small and medium-sized business

A very special standard prepared by the IASB is its *IFRS for SMEs*. There is a chapter devoted to this later (Chapter 7). Essentially it stands to one side of the other IFRS and is intended to be a stand-alone, complete set of accounting standards for small and medium-sized business. It aims to cover most transactions that a simpler company might be likely to encounter and was drafted with a company with about 50 employees in mind – not that small!

When a country mandates the use of IFRS, this does not include the SME standard; however, some countries – such as the UK – are planning to use it for all but the smallest privately held companies. The rules are very similar to IFRS but there are some simplifications. The standard also includes a cut-down conceptual framework.

Conclusion

Convergence on a single set of high quality accounting standards has been a key theme in the first decade of the century – which is probably why you are reading this book. Convergence brings lots of benefits for multinational companies and goes a step further towards an easily accessible global capital market. It makes raising capital cheaper and should give investors wider choices. It simplifies international transactions both within groups and by groups.

Convergence ... simplifies international transactions both within groups and by groups

The cost of transition may be high, and the benefits may not be reaped by all who have to bear the cost. In addition, application of the standards may not be uniform, even though standard-setters, stock exchange regulators and auditing firms have made a significant effort to reduce difference interpretations.

CHAPTER 2

CONTENT OF FINANCIAL STATEMENTS

This chapter introduces the standard collection of statements that are required on an annual basis under IFRS. The chapter reviews each of the main statements, the Statement of Comprehensive Income, the Statement of Financial Position and the Statement of Cash Flows. It goes on to discuss the factors that guide the choice of accounting policies and accounting policy change. After that it discusses fair presentation and finally interim financial statements. The chapter ends with an appendix that introduces the IASB Conceptual Framework.

The next six chapters will introduce you to the technical content of IFRS. They are organized by theme, starting with the presentation of accounting statements. Later chapters will deal with business combinations, income statement items, balance sheet line items, how to make accounting policy choices and first time adoption of IFRS.

The first thing to address is the confusing names that abound in the international standard-setting world. Firstly the standards themselves go under two different names. Those issued between 1973 and 2001 are called 'International Accounting Standards' (IAS), and those issued after that are called 'International Financial Reporting Standards' (IFRS). The difference is a semantic one: some people think that the standards do not refer to accounting (defined as the way a company organizes information in its accounting database) but rather to the way it draws up its financial statements. Other people think the difference is artificial – the annual statements are also referred to as annual accounts, and the way you organize your database is usually going to be to deliver efficiently the information you need for the financial statements. There is no difference in substance between IAS and IFRS, the only difference is that the latter were drawn up by a professional board, while the former were drawn up by (experienced) volunteers.

> **There is no difference in substance between IAS and IFRS**

The standards are backed up by 'Interpretations', which are issued by an expert committee to clarify something in a standard or whether a standard applies to a particular situation. Here again there have been name changes. The first committee was the Standard Interpretations Committee and its Interpretations were numbered, for example, 'SIC 12'. This was replaced by the International Financial Reporting Interpretations Committee, whose Interpretations are numbered IFRIC 12, etc. In 2010 this committee had its name changed to the IFRS Interpretations Committee. Interpretations have exactly the same force as IFRS. They do, though, disappear over time. The standard-setter incorporates Interpretations into the substantive standard when that standard is revised. So SIC 12, which deals with special purpose entities and is an Interpretation of IAS 27 *Consolidated and Separate Financial Statements* will disappear into IFRS 10 in 2011 when IAS 27 is replaced.

The official generic term that encompasses IAS, IFRS, SIC and IFRIC is 'IFRS'. So when in this book we refer to 'IFRS' we mean all the authoritative literature of international standards.

It should be borne in mind that IFRS have been written to be applied in financial statements intended for the capital markets. These are presumed to be **consolidated** or group statements. Listed companies consist rarely if ever of a single company, not least because it is much easier for tax and administrative purposes to have different legal entities in each country where the entity is active. They are usually therefore constituted as a set of different companies controlled by a parent or holding company. It is the holding company that is listed on one or more stock exchanges, and IFRS are designed to apply to the combined statements of the group. They can be, and are, applied to individual companies, but it remains a project for the future to review each standard to incorporate special provisions for individual company statements.

The names of the institutions that surround IFRS are just as confusing as those for the literature. The original standard-setter (1973–2000) was the Board of the International Accounting Standards Committee (IASC). In 2000–2001 there was a re-organization and a new professional board was created: the International Accounting Standards Board (IASB). However, this is a free-standing non-governmental organization and a Delaware Foundation was created and trustees appointed. Their job is to appoint members of the IASB but also to raise about $30m a year to support its operations. The Foundation was called the IASC Foundation, and changed its name to the IFRS Foundation in 2010. You'll be glad to know that the IASB has not changed its name recently.

That raises another point, which is that IFRS are always in a state of permanent evolution. For example, the G20 government leaders mandated the IASB and the US standard-setter to converge their standards by the end of 2011, which means that a number of major projects are being rammed through the system and will introduce significant changes in subsequent years.

Leaving aside that artificial pressure, and the need to revise financial instrument standards in particular as a result of the financial crisis, generally it takes a long time to write standards. You need typically three years to revise an existing standard and five to seven years to write a completely new one. The IASB does this in a transparent way (which is one reason why it takes a long time) so you see the changes coming from a long way off. However, the fact that you can see the changes coming means you live in a permanent state of expecting change. In the course of the following chapters there will be frequent references to forthcoming change. That is part of the world of IFRS.

IAS 1 presentation of financial statements

This standard has been revised many times, and continues to be revised, although it will likely be replaced in 2012 or 2013 but not for application until some time after that. It is the standard of reference for the presentation of financial statements and some key disclosures. While IAS 1 does not explicitly declare this, the ultimate objective of IFRS, as laid out in its Conceptual Framework[1], is to provide useful information to investors for making investment decisions. This is particularly relevant to the financial statements in that they try to distinguish the ongoing business from value changes and other changes in the business to help investors make their projections of future performance.

The standard does refer to users in the definition of materiality. It says that omissions or misstatements are material if they could influence the economic decisions of users. It adds that users are assumed to have a reasonable knowledge of business activities and accounting and a willingness to study the information provided in the financial statements with due diligence.

The standard provides that a complete set of financial statements consists of:

- Statement of Comprehensive Income
- Statement of Financial Position
- Statement of Changes in Equity

---

1 *Framework for the Preparation and Presentation of Financial Statements*, discussed in the appendix to this chapter.

- Statement of Cash Flows
- Notes to the accounts.

The financial statements must always include previous year comparative figures. The names of the statements have been harmonized with those in use by the US standard-setter in order to reduce differences. However, the Statement of Financial Position is commonly referred to as the Balance Sheet, and the IASB does not insist that the IAS 1 terms are used. In the US, what the IASB calls notes to the accounts are often referred to as the 'footnotes' – although in editorial parlance they are more properly described as 'end notes'. In mainland Europe the notes are sometimes referred to in translation as the Appendix or the Annex.

The Statement of Changes in Equity is not traditionally a financial statement as such in many countries, but is rather a note disclosure. In IFRS this statement shows changes in equity deriving from transactions with owners plus the change in comprehensive income for the year.

Statement of Comprehensive Income

To the newcomer to IFRS, this is probably the strangest part of the financial reporting package. To oversimplify, this is the traditional income statement or profit and loss account, with an extra bit added on at the bottom to show value changes. The Statement of Comprehensive Income is therefore:

Profit and Loss Account (Transactions)
+/– Other Comprehensive Income (Unrealized value changes)
= Total Comprehensive Income.

IAS 1 allows companies to show the Profit and Loss and Other Comprehensive Income on two separate pages. Some standard-setters object to this, but many companies think that the nature of the information in each part is different, and it misleads investors to put them together.

Comprehensive income is based on the idea that the key issue in accounting recognition and measurement is the assets and liabilities. At an extreme, one would, at each balance sheet date, measure the assets and liabilities and the difference between them would be equity. The difference in equity from one balance sheet to the next is comprehensive income. This gives you:

$Assets^1 - Liabilities^1 = Equity^1$
$Assets^2 - Liabilities^2 = Equity^2$
$\Delta\, Assets - \Delta\, Liabilities = \Delta\, Equity = $ Total Comprehensive Income for the reporting period.

And then, in order to understand the company's value generating activities better:

Total Comprehensive Income = Completed trading transactions + value changes.

In practice that theoretical position does not break down in such a straightforward way. Some financial instruments are valued at the price the entity could get in the current market value if sold as at balance sheet date (called 'fair value' in IFRS), and the value gain or loss on some of these instruments is treated as a profit and loss item as though it were a completed transaction. Similarly, traditional questions like inventory that has to be written down because you cannot sell the goods, would also be treated as a trading item, not a value change.

As very often in accounting, you can see an underlying idea, but in practice standard-setters have to make exceptions. With the inventory question, you can see that the loss is a result of a wrong trading decision, not an external value change that may be temporary in nature.

Putting an item in Other Comprehensive Income is not a choice open to the company when it draws up its accounts, it is something mandated by accounting standards. Currently the items that would go through there would include foreign exchange gains and losses arising from converting the financial statements of foreign subsidiaries into the reporting currency, some fair value gains and losses arising from valuing financial instruments at fair value at balance sheet date, valuation changes arising from carrying tangible and intangible non-current assets at valuation, and actuarial gains and losses arising from defined benefit pension schemes (value changes from the pension fund). This last is optional at the moment but will likely become the required treatment in 2012.

in practice standard-setters have to make exceptions

IAS 1 mandates a minimum set of line items on the face of the profit and loss (also called 'income statement'). This includes revenue, finance items and profit and loss on associates accounted for under the equity method, as well as the net profit or loss on discontinued businesses. It also provides recommended disclosures of further detail, including an analysis of expenses by function (cost of sales, marketing expense, administration, etc.) or by nature (employment costs, purchases of goods and materials for re-sale, depreciation, etc.). The income and expense are shown before tax, with tax shown as a deduction after the financial items. This profit figure is then split between that attributable to non-controlling interests (minority shareholders in subsidiaries) and that belonging to the shareholders in the parent company. Tables 1 and 2 illustrate a sample income statement and a Statement of Comprehensive Income.

IAS 1.85 says that an entity should present additional line items, headings and subtotals where it considers that these are relevant to its financial position. In the ACCOR statement in Table 1, you can see that the company has taken advantage of that to treat restructuring costs and impairments as 'non-recurring'. IFRS do not have an 'extraordinary' category of item omitted from operating profit.

Table 1 Consolidated income statements

(in million of euros)	Notes	2008*	2009
Revenue		7,593	6,971
Other operating revenue		129	94
CONSOLIDATED REVENUE	3	**7,722**	**7,065**
Operating expense	4	(5,432)	(5,089)
EBITDAR	5	**2,290**	**1,976**
Rental expense	6	(903)	(884)
EBITDA	7	**1,387**	**1,092**
Depreciation, amortization and provision expense	8	(446)	(498)
EBIT	9	**941**	**594**
Net financial expense	10	(86)	(143)
Share of profit of associates after tax	11	20	(3)
OPERATING PROFIT BEFORE TAX AND NON-RECURRING ITEMS		875	448
Restructuring costs	12	(56)	(127)
Impairment losses	13	(57)	(387)
Gains and losses on management of hotel properties	14	111	7
Gains and losses on management of other assets	15	13	(85)
OPERATING PROFIT BEFORE TAX		886	(144)
Income tax expense	16	(273)	(121)
Profit or loss from discontinued operations		–	–
NET PROFIT		613	(265)
Net Profit, Group Share		575	(282)
Net Profit, Minority interests	26	38	17
Weighted average number of shares outstanding *(in thousands)*	24	221,237	222,890
EARNINGS PER SHARE (in euros)		**2.60**	**(1.27)**
Diluted earnings per share *(in euros)*	24	2.59	(1.26)
Earnings per share from continuing operations *(in euros)*		**2.60**	**(1.27)**
Diluted earnings per share from continuing operations *(in euros)*		**2.59**	**(1.26)**
Earnings per share from discontinued operations *(in euros)*		N/A	N/A
Diluted earnings per share from discontinued operations *(in euros)*		N/A	N/A

Source: ACCOR SA financial statements 2009.

*Adjusted for the effects of the change of method described in Note 1 concerning customer loyalty programmes.

Table 2 Statements of comprehensive income

(in million of euros)	Notes	2008*	2009
NET PROFIT		**613**	**(265)**
Currency translation adjustment		(267)	167
Change in fair value resulting from 'Available-for-sale financial assets'		1	–
Effective portion of gains and losses on hedging instruments in a cash flow hedge		(6)	(6)
Actuarial gains and losses on defined benefits plans		(4)	(3)
Share of the other comprehensive income of associates and joint ventures accounted for using the equity method		–	–
Other comprehensive income, net of tax	27	**(276)**	**158**
TOTAL COMPREHENSIVE INCOME		**337**	**(107)**
Comprehensive income, Group share		**344**	**(127)**
Comprehensive income, Minority interests		(7)	20

Source: ACCOR SA financial statements 2009.

Statement of Financial Position

IAS 1 *Presentation of Financial Statements* does not prescribe a detailed layout for the balance sheet (Statement of Financial Position) either. It identifies a series of line items that must be included where relevant. The only rules are that the default format distinguishes between **current** and **non-current** items. As an exception to this presentation rule, where an entity believes it would give better information, the assets and liabilities may be organized according to liquidity.

In the nineteenth century, accountants referred to fixed assets (long-term capacity such as plant) and circulating assets (assets linked to the business cycle such as inventory and client accounts). Over time the circulating assets were relabelled current assets, and now the fixed assets have been relabelled 'non-current' by the international standard-setters.

A rule of thumb in financial reporting is that current assets usually convert to cash in less than a year while non-current assets convert in more than a year. This rather loose notion is made more specific in IFRS. IAS 1 uses the 'operating cycle' to distinguish between current and non-current items. The operating cycle is the time taken to complete a single cash to cash transformation in the company's business. In a manufacturing business, the first part of the cycle is to buy raw materials; these are then processed to create finished goods. The finished goods are sold, probably on credit, and when the client has paid for them, you are at the end of the cycle. Current items are generated within the operating cycle, and convert to cash as part of that cycle. Non-current items are not part of the cycle.

A current asset could have a conversion period of more than one year – for example, extended credit to a privileged client, or slow-moving inventory. In this case it is still classified as current but the entity must identify the part that will convert in more than one year – this is usually done in the notes. Similarly, non-current items could convert in less than a year. A term loan that matures in the next 12 months would be an example. Again the classification is respected but the short-term nature of the item is disclosed either on the face of the accounts or in the notes.

While the traditional non-current balance sheet line items such as intangible and financial assets are required, IAS 1 mandates a separate line for biological assets. It also specifies property plant and equipment, and investment property as separate lines, rather than a single tangible asset line. Investments accounted for using the equity method must be split out of financial assets. The changes in equity-accounted investments do not reflect cash flows; they reflect the accounting value of the associate as opposed to cost or market value. IAS 1 makes the point elsewhere that generally where one class of assets is measured on a different basis from another similar class, this is a reason for disclosing them separately.

There is also a special line item for assets held for disposal (we will look at this later – the essence is that once an entity decides to sell part of its business, the operating results are shown separately in profit and loss and the assets and liabilities are also shown separately – and may be treated as a 'disposal group').

IAS 1 specifies that current tax should be shown separately from deferred tax. Trade and other payables should be shown separately from other financial liabilities. Provisions (probably due to become 'non-financial liabilities') should also be a separate line item. Probably the most striking issue on the financing side of the balance sheet is that non-controlling interests (also known outside IFRS as 'minority interests' – shares in group subsidiaries held by people or entities outside the group) are shown within group equity. In many jurisdictions these would have been shown as a separate line item, usually between liabilities and equity. The emphasis would be put on the 'equity' number relating only to the interests of shareholders in the parent company. Tables 3 (assets) and 4 (liabilities and equity) illustrate a sample consolidated balance sheet.

Table 3 Consolidated balance sheets: assets

(in million of euros)	Notes	Jan 1, 2008*	Dec 2008*	Dec 2009
GOODWILL	17	1,967	1,932	1,777
INTANGIBLE ASSETS	18	369	512	488
PROPERTY, PLANT AND EQUIPMENT	19	3,321	4,324	4,306
Long-term loans	20	107	78	107
Investments in associates	21	421	176	191
Other financial investments	22	182	149	130
TOTAL NON-CURRENT FINANCIAL ASSETS		710	403	428
Deferred tax assets	16	203	226	291
TOTAL NON-CURRENT ASSETS		**6,570**	**7,397**	**7,290**
Inventories		74	103	60
Trade receivables	23	1,598	1,313	1,350
Other receivables and accruals	23	715	824	1,113
Prepaid services voucher reserve funds	392	441	565	
Receivables on disposals of assets	28 & 29	52	16	43
Short-term loans	28 & 29	22	34	17
Cash and cash equivalents	28 & 29	1,138	1,253	1,164
TOTAL CURRENT ASSETS		**3,991**	**3,984**	**4,312**
Assets held for sale	31	277	36	144
TOTAL ASSETS		**10,838**	**11,417**	**11,746**

Source: ACCOR SA financial statements 2009.
*Adjusted for the effects of the change of method described in Note 1 concerning customer loyalty programmes.

Table 4 Consolidated balance sheets: equity and liabilities

(in million of euros)	Notes	Jan 1, 2008*	Dec. 2008*	Dec. 2009
Share capital		665	660	676
Additional paid-in capital		2,276	2,226	2,379
Retained earnings		(102)	151	363
Hedging instruments reserve	25	–	(6)	(12)
Fair value adjustments on financial instruments reserve	25	66	–	–
Reserve for actuarial gains/losses		(19)	(23)	(26)
Reserve related to employee benefits		59	82	102
Currency translation reserve		(145)	(367)	(203)
Net profit, Group share		883	575	(282)
SHAREHOLDERS' EQUITY, GROUP SHARE	24	3,683	3,298	2,997
Minority interests	26	61	258	257
TOTAL SHAREHOLDERS' EQUITY AND MINORITY INTERESTS		3,744	3,556	3,254
Other long-term financial debt	28 & 29	1,056	1,927	2,332
Long-term finance lease liabilities	28 & 29	216	161	143
Deferred tax liabilities	16	170	199	211
Non-current provisions	32	118	131	132
TOTAL NON-CURRENT LIABILITIES		**5,304**	**5,974**	**6,072**
Trade payables	23	679	765	709
Other payables and income tax payable	23	1,569	1,613	1,463
Prepaid services voucher in circulation		2,894	2,587	2,883
Current provisions	32	248	191	242
Short-term debt and finance lease liabilities	28 & 29	109	165	285
Bank overdrafts	28 & 29	35	122	88
TOTAL CURRENT LIABILITIES		**5,534**	**5,443**	**5,670**
Liabilities of assets classified as held for sale	31	–	–	4
TOTAL LIABILITIES AND SHAREHOLDERS' EQUITY		**10,838**	**11,417**	**11,746**

Source: ACCOR SA financial statements 2009.

*Adjusted for the effects of the change of method described in Note 1 concerning customer loyalty programmes.

Statement of Cash Flows

While IAS 1 provides that a Statement of Cash Flows is part of the reporting package, this statement has its own standard, IAS 7 *Statement of Cash Flows*. This is one of the few standards that the IASB has not been tempted to tinker with in recent years, although it too will ultimately be replaced in the financial statement presentation joint project with the FASB (Financial Accounting Standards Board). It was also the first standard to be accepted by the SEC as equivalent to the US standard on the subject.

IAS 7 follows the usual analysis of cash flows over:

- operating activities
- investing activities
- financing activities.

The aggregate of these three has to be shown to be equal to the movement in cash and cash equivalents from balance sheet to balance sheet. 'Cash equivalents' is defined as near-liquid instruments that are expected to convert to cash in less than three months. It is likely that the replacement standard will eliminate the cash equivalents. Foreign currency translation differences that impact the carrying value of cash and cash equivalents are shown as an adjustment to the movement in cash balances.

This [IAS 7 Statement of Cash Flows] was the first standard to be accepted by the SEC

The standard requires that tax, interest and dividends be separately identified in the statement of cash flows. It suggests that taxation would normally go under operating activities, but leaves entities a free choice for interest and dividends, received and paid. Transactions that do not involve cash are not included in the statement. This means that, for example, the acquisition of another entity for shares would be excluded from the analysis. Where an entity holds investments that are measured using the equity method, only the dividends received from these would be shown in the statement of cash flows.

A sample of consolidated cash flow statements is shown in Table 5.

Table 5 Consolidated cash flow statements

(in million of euros)	Notes	2008*	2009
+ EBITDA	7	1,387	1,092
− Net financial expense	10	(86)	(143)
− Income tax expense		(277)	(161)
− Non-cash revenue and expense included in EBITDA		38	32
−			
Elimination of provision movements included in net financial expense, income tax expense and non-recurring taxes		41	19
+ Dividends received from associates		8	4
= FUNDS FROM ORDINARY ACTIVITIES	33	1,111	843
+ Decrease (increase) in operating working capital	34	25	(61)**
= NET CASH FROM OPERATING ACTIVITIES		1,137	781
+			
Cash received (paid) on non-recurring transactions (included restructuring costs and non-recurring taxes)		(86)	(156)
+ Decrease (increase) in non-operating working capital	34	–	(242)
=			
NET CASH FROM OPERATING ACTIVITIES INCLUDING NON-RECURRING TRANSACTIONS (A)		1,050	383
− Renovation and maintenance expenditure	35	(488)	(327)
− Development expenditure	36	(1,091)	(766)
+ Proceeds from disposals of assets		560	363
= NET CASH USED IN INVESTMENTS/DIVESTMENTS (B)		(1,019)	(730)

+ Proceeds from issue of share capital	***	8	175
– Capital reduction		(62)	–
– Dividends paid		(719)	(396)
– Repayment of long-term debt		(781)	(1,253)
– Payment of finance lease liabilities		(65)	(8)
+ New long-term debt		1,742	1,842
= INCREASE (DECREASE) IN LONG-TERM DEBT		896	581
+ Increase (decrease) in short-term debt		23	(33)
= NET CASH FROM FINANCING ACTIVITIES (C)		146	327
– EFFECT OF CHANGES IN EXCHANGE RATES (D)		(140)	(28)
= NET CHANGE IN CASH AND CASH EQUIVALENTS **(E)=(A)+(B)+(C)+(D)**	29	**37**	**(48)**
+ Cash and cash equivalents at beginning of period		1,103	1,131
+ Effect of changes in fair value of cash and cash equivalents		(9)	(7)
– Cash and cash equivalents at end of period		1,131	1,076
= NET CHANGE IN CASH AND CASH EQUIVALENTS	29	**37**	**(48)**

Source: ACCOR SA financial statements 2009.

*Adjusted for the effects of the change of method described in Note 1 concerning customer loyalty programmes.

(**)

Decrease (increase) in operating working capital – Prepaid Services. 111
Decrease (increase) in operating working capital – Hospitality. (58)
Reclassification from cash and cash equivalents to restricted cash. (114)
Total decrease (increase) in operating working capital. (61)
***Including stock dividends paid in 2009 for €162 million.

Statement of Changes in Equity

The statement of changes in equity must show a reconciliation between the opening and closing amounts of each class of equity (what the FASB would call a 'roll forward'), separating out the effects of retrospective changes in accounting policies, profit and loss, and other comprehensive income, as well as transactions with owners. In many countries this sort of information is often provided in the notes to the accounts.

Accounting policies and changes

IAS 1 *Presentation of Financial Statements* says that companies should present a full discussion of accounting policies and this would normally start with an 'explicit and unreserved statement' of compliance with IFRS, which is then followed by a presentation of the significant accounting policy choices made.

The 'explicit and unreserved statement' is a controversial issue that has a lot of baggage. In the 1990s some companies, particularly French ones, used to comply only with selected standards. They used to specify that their statements were drawn up in compliance with international standards – but with exceptions. Frequently they did not comply with the pensions' standard (IAS 19) and many did not make the disclosures of the remuneration of key personnel mandated by IAS 24. Such usage came to be referred to as 'IAS lite' and was considered to bring the international standards into disrepute. IAS 1 was therefore reformulated at the end of the decade to include this requirement that an entity could only refer to international standards if it was in full compliance and made an explicit and unreserved statement to that effect.

However, the situation was then complicated by the EU. For IFRS to be mandatory in the EU, they have to be voted into European law. This unfortunately provides an opportunity for entities that are not happy with a particular standard to try to persuade participants in the EU endorsement system to delete parts of the standard (known as a 'carve-out'). This has so far only happened once, in relation to a detailed issue on financial instruments that affects only banks and similar institutions, even though it has been threatened more often. However, EU listed companies are supposed to state in their policy note that they comply with IFRS 'as endorsed by the European Union', which as a consequence are not exactly the same as IFRS as issued by the IASB.

The IASB did consider further amending IAS 1 to require that where an entity could not assert full compliance, it should be explicit about what was the difference. However, there was a lot of opposition to this as opening the door to non-compliance, so it was dropped. A further complication is that while the SEC recognizes IFRS as equivalent to US GAAP for foreign registrants, and therefore does not require costly reconciliation to US GAAP numbers, this recognition applies only to IFRS as issued by the IASB. Consequently a European listed company that is also an SEC registrant, has – if it wishes to claim the privileges that the SEC gives to IFRS – to specify that it complies with IFRS as endorsed by the EU **and** IFRS as issued by the IASB.

For IFRS to be mandatory in the EU, they have to be voted into European law

IAS 1 says that the entity must disclose the judgements that it has made that have the most significant impact upon the accounting policies. It must also disclose assumptions and other sources of accounting uncertainty that have a significant risk of causing material adjustments in due course. This disclosure was added as a result of the Enron scandal. Part of the Enron manipulations involved assumptions about future energy prices and their impact on the fair value of energy supply contracts, giving rise to unrealized fair value gains included in the profits.

The choice of accounting policies is addressed in IAS 8 *Accounting Policies, Changes in Accounting Estimates and Errors*. This provides a hierarchy which says that in looking for a policy for a particular class of transactions, the entity should:

(1) look at the standards and interpretations
(2) if the transaction is not specifically mentioned, look to analogize to a similar transaction in the standards and interpretations
(3) if that is unsuccessful, look to the conceptual framework for guidance
(4) look to the accounting standards of national standard-setters that have a similar conceptual framework.

There are a number of implications of this hierarchy. As regards analogies, when the IFRS Interpretations Committee is asked to take a position on an issue, one of the questions it asks itself is whether it is creating a precedent that would be analogized to in different circumstances. Both the Interpretations Committee and the IASB itself on occasion will consider whether they are creating unexpected opportunities and will specify if a treatment is exceptional and should not be analogized to.

The use of the conceptual framework as the next level has the effect of making the framework virtually part of GAAP, which is not the case in the US. Where a transaction is not addressed in IFRS, the entity can determine its own treatment as long as it can be justified in terms of the framework (dealt with below).

Finally, the reference to national standards (the last alternative in the hierarchy) could have the impact of switching (say) a European company into US GAAP. For this reason its use has been suspended in IFRS 4 *Insurance Contracts* and IFRS 6 *Exploration for and Evaluation of Mineral Resources*, pending the development of international standards on such subjects. However, if the US decided to adopt IFRS, this would mean that where a US standard addressed something that was not covered in IFRS (and there are many sector-specific standards in the US that have no IFRS counterpart), the US standards would continue to apply.

IAS 8 also deals with changes in accounting policies. As IFRS are apt to change fairly frequently, this is a relevant issue. In principle, IAS 8 says that a new IFRS should be applied retrospectively (as though it had always applied) and any changes in accounting values already reported should be taken as a one-time adjustment in equity. In Europe particularly, national Commercial Codes often do not allow such a treatment – the published closing balance sheet of one year is inviolate and any changes have to be shown in the current year.

A particularity of IFRS is that where an accounting policy change is applied retrospectively, the entity must produce a re-stated opening balance sheet for the periods reported. So if the entity reported the current year and a comparative year, it would produce three balance sheets – one for the opening of the comparative year, and one each at the end of the two years reported.

Retrospective application may, however, be modified by the transitional rules of new standards. In particular, the IASB will not mandate retrospective application if it involves making estimates or determining fair values with the benefit of hindsight. There is also a general exception for impracticability – defined as not being able to do something after having made every reasonable effort.

Fair presentation

IAS 1 says that the statements must present fairly the financial position, financial performance and cash flows of the entity. It specifies that it is presumed that this will be achieved by compliance with IFRS. However, it does allow that 'in extremely rare circumstances' an entity may decide that compliance would not result in a fair presentation, and in such circumstances it may depart from individual standards. If it does this, it must explain why and show the effect on the financial statements.

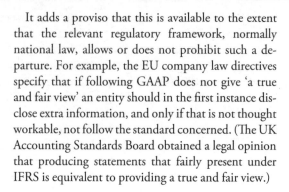

the statements must present fairly the financial position, financial performance and cash flows of the entity

It adds a proviso that this is available to the extent that the relevant regulatory framework, normally national law, allows or does not prohibit such a departure. For example, the EU company law directives specify that if following GAAP does not give 'a true and fair view' an entity should in the first instance disclose extra information, and only if that is not thought workable, not follow the standard concerned. (The UK Accounting Standards Board obtained a legal opinion that producing statements that fairly present under IFRS is equivalent to providing a true and fair view.)

Conventions

IAS 1 also mentions the regular accounting conventions of going concern, consistency and accruals (leaving aside the cash flow statement). There is no mention of prudence, though. The standard also discusses the issue of materiality and aggregation, saying that each material class of similar items should be presented separately. There is a prohibition on offsetting assets and liabilities and income and expenses, unless a specific IFRS requires it, as is the case in IAS 20 *Accounting for Government Grants and Disclosure of Government Assistance*. The US does permit offsetting of derivatives, and this remains an area for convergence. It is discussed further in Chapter 8, which focuses on differences between IFRS and US GAAP.

Interim financial statements

The IASB does not require companies to produce financial statements other than on an annual basis, but it does have a standard, IAS 34 *Interim Financial Reporting*, that tells IFRS companies what is the minimum information that should be in interim statements, in circumstances where national law or stock exchange regulations require the production of three-monthly or six-monthly figures.

Essentially the minimum set of documents (IAS 34.8) should be:

- condensed statement of financial position
- condensed statement of comprehensive income
- condensed statement of cash flows
- condensed statement of changes in equity
- selected notes.

The standard does not 'discourage' people from providing full statements, but where condensed ones are used, says these should preserve the main headings and subtotals of the full annual statements. The objective in interim reports should be (IAS 34. 6):

> to provide an update on the latest complete set of annual financial statements. Accordingly, it focuses on new activities, events, and circumstances and does not duplicate information previously reported.

However, the standard does include a long list of the minimum footnotes that should be provided, including a statement that accounting policies are the same as in the annual statements, limited segment information and comments on any seasonality in the group's business. The statements must include comparative information. For the balance sheet this is the immediately preceding annual balance sheet, but for the statement of comprehensive income and statement of cash flows, this is the previous year's figures for the comparable period. It suggests that if there are significant seasonal variations, the full year comparatives might be given as well.

The standard has been criticized in the past by the IASB for its lack of clarity. In 2006 an Interpretation (IFRIC 10) was issued on the treatment of goodwill impairment in relation to interim accounts. The question was whether, given that goodwill had been impaired in the first interim statements (but the situation had improved before the end of the financial year), the impairment could be reversed. The Interpretations Committee's answer was that the impairment could not be reversed, because the second six months was a subsequent accounting period in terms of the IFRS literature.

IAS 34 *Interim Financial Reporting* is not crystal clear on the fundamental issue of whether the interim period should be treated as a discrete period, or part of the full year. It specifies a 'year to date' approach, without explaining what that means. If we take as an illustration the example of carrying out an extensive, non-routine, maintenance operation on plant in the first half year, costing €12m. The question is: should you (1) report that as €6m of expense in each half year (i.e. treating the half year as integral to the annual result); or (2) take a €12m expense in the first half results (a discrete reporting period)? The IFRS Interpretations Committee was inclined to the second view, although the Interpretation also said that this decision should not be analogized for other IAS 34 issues.

The view expressed when the IASB was debating whether to approve the Interpretation, was that IAS 34 is a flawed standard that needs to be tidied up. However, the Board did not expect to have time to address it as it was concentrating on its convergence programme. It could be a standard that is revisited in the post 2011 programme.

Conclusion

This chapter has presented an analysis of the IFRS requirements for the form and content of financial statements, including interim statements. It has attempted to draw attention to those areas where IFRS requirements differ from what might be expected in traditional, national practice.

Appendix: The IASB Conceptual Framework

As has been touched on in the chapter on presentation, the IASB has a Conceptual Framework, *The Framework for Preparation and Presentation of Financial Statements*. The original was passed in 1989 and it is, like all other anglophone conceptual frameworks for accounting, based on the US model. There is one significant difference in the status of the two documents. The FASB concepts statements were explicitly drawn up to guide the formulation of standards, and are for the use of standard-setters only.

In terms of the politics of US standard-setting, a criticism made of the FASB's predecessor was that standards did not have any unifying logic and standard-setters were thought to make pragmatic decisions based potentially on private interests. The conceptual framework was intended to provide a structure for decisions. The FASB conceptual framework does not constitute authoritative literature for preparers and auditors.

The IASB framework, however, issued a decade later in a different context, acknowledges the need for a structure but also uses it to inform the choice of accounting policies by preparers. Gilbert Gélard, a member of the IASB from 2001 to 2010, points out that IFRS must provide standards that are not jurisdiction-specific and are more principles-based. In these circumstances it is necessary to provide guidance to companies as how to interpret the standards to fit specific circumstances.

In 2004 the IASB embarked on a joint programme with the FASB to converge and improve their conceptual frameworks. It is a logical step that if the two standard-setters want to converge their standards, they should necessarily converge the conceptual framework on which the standards are based – even if their existing frameworks have no significant differences. The update and convergence programme is expected to take a long time, and is more a question of fine-tuning the existing material and extending it where it lacks detail (such as measurement, and defining the reporting entity) than making any substantive changes. Two key chapters were issued in final form in 2010: the *Objectives of Financial Reporting* and the *Qualitative Characteristics of Financial Reporting*. (There is a subtle change here: the new literature talks about financial reporting, not financial statements. The implication is that the standard-setters might extend slightly the scope of their mandate.)

The objective of financial reporting is given as:

> *The objective of general purpose financial reporting is to provide financial information about the reporting entity that is useful to present and potential equity investors, lenders and other creditors in making decisions in their capacity as capital providers. Information that is decision-useful to capital providers may also be useful to other users of financial reporting who are not capital providers.*

(Objectives of Financial Reporting, OB2)

This can be summed up as saying that IFRS (and US standards) should provide information that is 'decision-useful' to capital providers. People often talk about IFRS as having an 'investor perspective' – the standards are formulated on the assumption that their main purpose is to feed into the decision-making in the public capital markets.

This might imply that information in the financial statements is only useful if it feeds into decisions about the future. The original US statement did indeed talk about investment decisions. The new version talks about decisions 'as capital providers' to reflect the fact that the original IASB document considered that stewardship, or accountability for past actions, was an end in itself. The supporting paragraphs explain that the statements should cover both aspects. Some standard-setters think that you cannot in any event distinguish between them.

The chapter notes that capital providers are interested in assessing the 'amount, timing and uncertainty' of cash flows, which presumably refers to forecasting this. It makes the point that the investor is interested in dividends, interest and eventual sale or redemption of securities, and implicitly these are the cash flows the investor is trying to estimate. So while the investor may be trying to estimate the entity's ability to generate future cash, the investor's interest in that is only because of the effect it has on the value of the entity's securities and its ability to pay dividends and interest. The financial statements should show the resources available to the entity and the claims upon those resources.

The IASB emphasize that their standards concern 'general purpose financial reporting' – that is, financial statements issued for public use (for people who cannot require the company to prepare information directly). They make the distinction on the basis that other statements may be issued for special purposes (for example, in support of profit-sharing or royalty arrangements, or for tax), and presumably that company law and other regulatory constraints address only general purpose financial statements.

The other point is that while more general analyses of the users of public financial statements identify other interests such as clients, suppliers, staff, government, public interest bodies, etc., the IASB and FASB concentrate exclusively on capital providers. Indeed, in many countries the whole basis of the legal regulation of reporting is to provide information for, and protection of, shareholders and creditors. The Objectives do not ignore other users, but take the view that information that satisfies shareholders, who are the ultimate bearers of corporate risk, should be useful to people whose risk is less.

Qualitative characteristics

The qualitative characteristics of financial reporting fall into three categories: fundamental, enhancing and constraints. The fundamental characteristics are relevance and representational faithfulness. Relevance is analysed as being capable of making a difference to a decision by a capital provider. This could mean it is confirmatory (e.g. provides feedback on past estimates) or has predictive value (e.g. helps with current estimates of the future). The literature notes that information can be capable of making a difference even if does not in the end do so.

The financial statements should be portraying the resources of the entity and claims on those resources, as well as transactions that affect resources and claims. Information must be a faithful representation of those economic phenomena. This means that it should be 'complete, neutral and free from material error'. The chapter makes clear that information should reflect the economic substance and not necessarily the legal form. It can be argued that the 'neutral' qualification is at odds with a traditional view that accounting measurement should be 'prudent' – but individual standard-setters point out that prudence or conservatism builds in an implicit bias that diminishes the value of the information. The chapter notes that relevance should first be applied to see what information would be decision-useful, and then from the range available, the most representationally faithful should be chosen (during the drafting of the updates, the staff made several attempts to construct a flow chart to show how the qualitative characteristics should be applied, but gave up in the end).

The second category is 'enhancing characteristics' – those which when present enhance the decision-usefulness of information that is relevant and representationally faithful. These are identified as comparability, verifiability, timeliness and understandability. Comparability is the characteristic that helps people identify similarities and differences. The chapter points out that this goal is served by consistency. Verifiability assumes that knowledgeable people could reach a consensus that the information is representationally faithful.

Understandability is self-explanatory, but there is general disagreement among different groups as to what level of knowledge a reader of financial statements might be expected to have. The chapter specifies:

> 'Users of financial reports are assumed to have a reasonable knowledge of business and economic activities and to be able to read a financial

report. In making decisions, users also should review and analyse the information with reasonable diligence.'

(Qualitative Characteristics QC24)

The application of these characteristics is limited by two pervasive constraints: materiality and cost. Information is deemed to be material if it could influence the decisions taken by investors (this is reflected in IAS 1). The cost constraint is that the benefits of providing the information must exceed the costs of producing that information. Both of these constraints are difficult to operationalize. Standard-setters tend to take the view that it is for them to make an assessment of the benefits and to decide whether these exceed the costs of supplying particular information. Individual preparers cannot really use the cost argument to justify departure from an obligation, but materiality is pervasive and the entity is free to make a judgement about that.

Materiality is a slightly tricky issue. Anecdotal evidence suggests that auditors are reluctant to allow companies to apply the materiality criterion. It is not referred to typically in individual standards, but the IASB quite often refers to it in debate. A recent example would be the leasing standard, where feedback was that people wanted an exception for small lease contracts. The IASB said you already have an exception if the contracts are not material. Asked to put a specific mention in the standard, they argued that materiality is a pervasive concept and if you mention it specifically in one standard that raises questions of whether it applies less in others.

Assets and liabilities
The conceptual framework identifies what it labels 'elements' of financial statements – the building blocks that together constitute the contents of the financial statements. The framework identifies assets, liabilities, equity, income and expenses. However, the motors of these are the definitions of asset and liability. As discussed above in relation

to comprehensive income and to the qualitative characteristics, the main focus of the statements for the standard-setter is identifying and measuring the company's resources (assets) and the claims on them (liabilities). Equity is the excess of assets over liabilities, and the changes in equity can be classified as income (increases equity) and expenses (decreases equity).

The definitions of asset and liability are therefore fundamental, and are applied by standard-setters when debating a new standard. An asset is:

> *A resource controlled by the entity as a result of past events and from which future economic benefits are expected to flow to the entity*
>
> (*Framework for the Preparation and Presentation of Financial Statements*, Para 49(a))

Whereas a liability is:

> *A present obligation of the entity arising from past events, the settlement of which is expected to result in an outflow from the entity of resources embodying economic benefits*
>
> (*Framework for the Preparation and Presentation of Financial Statements*, Para 49(b))

These definitions determine what constitutes an asset or liability of the entity, but they do not on their own satisfy the requirement for **recognition** in the financial statements. For an asset or liability to be recognized (i.e. appear in the financial statements) it must satisfy two criteria: the future cash flow must be **probable** (interpreted as more likely than not in IFRS); and it must be capable of being measured with reasonable certainty. The financial statements do not therefore necessarily reflect all the assets and liabilities of the entity. The boundary of the financial statements is set where cash flows become both probable and measurable.

A related issue is that the asset must be **controlled** by the entity to qualify for possible recognition. This means that certain types of assets, especially intangibles, are excluded from the financial statements. Things like staff know-how, the effects of an advertising campaign and customer loyalty, which all add to an entity's ability to generate cash flows, are excluded from the financial statements because they are not controlled by the entity. A sort of rough test that standard-setters apply in debating if there is an asset that should be recognized is to ask if you could sell it.

In the IASB/FASB update of their conceptual frameworks, the standard-setters have had many debates about revising these fundamental definitions but have so far failed to reach agreement on a new version that is robust. Two areas where they feel clarification is necessary are rights, and the ability to prevent access. The rights question is the more slippery – they ask whether the asset is the actual asset (e.g. a truck) or the right to use the asset. In most cases the answer doesn't matter but in other cases it may do. For example, if you purchased a forward contract to buy corn, is your asset the right to buy the corn, or the actual corn? The other issue is that sometimes assets are held not to exploit directly but to prevent other people exploiting. It is more tenuous in that case to identify the cash flows that the asset is expected to generate.

The parts of the conceptual framework discussed above are those that you are most likely to come across, and are useful in debating new standards. The conceptual framework does, however, address other issues such as measurement and the reporting entity. There is work continuing in these areas. As regards measurement, the standard-setters are developing material that will help to determine what kind of measurement basis is appropriate (e.g. current value, historical cost, replacement cost, etc.). This identifies that one of the ways in which assets differ from each other is the way in which they can generate cash flows. Some assets, such as investment properties, loans and finished goods, can generate cash flows on their own. They generate rental income, interest or can be sold. Other assets, however, have to be used in combinations to generate income. For example, a factory needs raw materials, plant, etc., to make finished goods that are then sold.

There is no discussion of the reporting entity in the original IASB conceptual framework. The staff are working on a definition that says the reporting entity is all the business that is controlled by a single management. This means that the only relevant financial statements are consolidated ones. The draft says that individual company financial statements cannot be 'general purpose financial statements' but they may have information that is useful to investors and may be issued with the consolidated statements but not on their own.

This appendix has aimed to give you a rapid analysis of the main aspects of the IASB conceptual framework. As discussed the framework can come into choice of accounting principles, but the main reason for presenting it here is that it provides insights into the orientation of IFRS.

CHAPTER 3

INVESTMENTS IN OTHER COMPANIES

This chapter reviews the standards dealing with consolidation and business combinations. It deals with the definition of control, which determines what companies are included as subsidiaries. It also looks at the rules for translation of the statements of foreign subsidiaries. It then looks at the standards on business combinations, associated companies, joint ventures and investments in equities. The chapter includes an appendix on fair value measurement.

As discussed in Chapter 2, the reporting entity is defined as all the businesses that are under a unified control. As a consequence IFRS financial statements are necessarily consolidated statements and must include all the other businesses in which the holding company has an interest. The way in which a company accounts for its investments in other companies is therefore fundamental to IFRS financial statements. In practice, this is covered in a series of different standards. Like many other things, this area is undergoing change and replacement standards should be in place with an application date around 2013. This chapter will deal with the standards currently in force, and then go on to outline the probable changes, which are more likely to affect disclosures than recognition and measurement.

Consolidation

IAS 27 *Consolidated and Separate Financial Statements* addresses the requirements for identifying subsidiaries and then consolidating their figures, while SIC 12 *Consolidation – Special Purpose Entities*, as its name implies, deals with special purpose entities (SPEs). The two will be replaced in 2011 by a new standard (IFRS10) which refines the rules without changing the main thrust of the requirements.

The key determinant of whether an investee company should be consolidated is whether they are controlled by the investor company. Control is defined by IAS 27 as 'the power to govern the financial and operating policies of an entity so as to obtain benefits from its activities'. The standard expands to say that control is presumed to exist when the investor has a majority of the voting shares and also:

(a) power over more than half of the voting rights by virtue of an agreement with other investors;
(b) power to govern the financial and operating policies of the entity under a statute or an agreement;
(c) power to appoint or remove the majority of the members of the board of directors or equivalent governing body and control of the entity is by that board or body; or
(d) power to cast the majority of votes at meetings of the board of directors or equivalent governing body and control of the entity is by that board or body.

The issue is also addressed in SIC 12, which says that an SPE should be consolidated 'when the substance of the relationship between an entity and the SPE indicates that the SPE is controlled by that entity'. The

Interpretation points to a range of situations where one company would be considered to control an SPE in substance. These include examples such as when the SPE is conducting its business in a way that meets the needs of the investor, or the investor company gets most of the benefits or is exposed to most of the risk of the SPE.

The standard does not go into much further detail about the ability to control, although there is implementation guidance on potential voting rights. Recent discussions with the FASB about producing a joint standard on consolidation have suggested that when the investor has less than 50% of the votes, the voting pattern at annual general meetings could be a factor to take into account. Supposing the investor owns 40% and the rest of the shares are spread through a large number of small shareholders, it is likely that the owner of the 40% block will in practice win all the motions at the AGM and nominate the board of directors. The argument is that if there is evidence that one investor exercises control, then they should consolidate. There is no requirement in IAS 27 that the investor should be able to perpetuate that control indefinitely.

The way in which a company accounts for its investments in other companies is ... fundamental to IFRS financial statements

IAS 27 points out that there may be equity instruments such as options or warrants which, if exercised, would ensure that one investor had control. The standard simply says that one must look at 'all the facts and circumstances' in deciding whether these affect the consolidation decision. This is an issue that standard-setters are divided on. Some consider that these instruments should be taken into account only once exercised, while others suggest that the threat of exercise may be sufficient to provide control. The standard says that they must be taken into account, and provides (non-mandatory) Implementation Guidance for assessing the situation.

Another grey area is consolidation by professional investment companies such as mutual funds, equity capital funds, etc. The standard says that anything that meets the definition of a subsidiary must be consolidated, irrespective of whether the investor is a venture capital company, unit trust or similar entity.

Where the controlling entity owns less than 100% of the shares, the share of net income attributable to outside shareholders has to be identified. The parent consolidates all the assets and liabilities but then shows the interest of the outside shareholders as a **non-controlling interest** (outside of IASB and FASB terminology this would be a 'minority interest'). A specificity of IFRS is that the non-controlling interests must be shown in the balance sheet as a line item within group equity. In many countries they are shown after group equity as a separate section of the financing side of the balance sheet.

Another issue with non-controlling interests is that where the subsidiary has been acquired as part of a business combination, there is a choice between showing the net assets related to non-controlling interests at their fair value at acquisition or their historical cost. The IASB wanted to require the non-controlling interests to be carried at fair value but when this was proposed there was a good deal of pushback from constituents, and so in the final version of IFRS 3 it is optional.

IAS 27 specifies that the consolidation procedure involves elimination of all intra-group balances, transactions, income and expense. The year-end dates of all subsidiaries and parent should be the same, or if not, additional statements should be prepared to reach the same date – although there is an impracticability exception. The accounting principles used in the consolidated statements must be uniform – but there is no requirement that these be the principles applied by the parent company.

Translation of foreign subsidiaries

Of course, a multinational company will have many, perhaps most, of its subsidiaries trading in a currency other than that of the parent.

Consequently there need to be rules for converting the financial statements into a single currency in order to produce consolidated statements. The standard that deals with this under IFRS is IAS 21 *The Effects of Changes in Exchange Rates*.

Before the oil price crisis in the 1970s many major currencies were managed by governments within a relatively fixed framework and large swings in exchange rates were relatively rare. However, as companies became more international they became exposed to a wider range of currencies. In addition, the oil price crisis triggered massive inflation, which in turn put pressure on exchange rates and governments mostly abandoned attempts to peg their rates and allowed them to float freely. One consequence of this was that converting (or 'translating') the statements of foreign subsidiaries started to throw up significant fluctuations year on year. In the US, under SFAS 8, these fluctuations were passed through the income statement, whereas in Europe they were mostly treated as temporary differences to be addressed in equity.

there need to be rules for converting the financial statements into a single currency ... to produce consolidated statements

A consequence of this was a major review of accounting for foreign currency transactions, which eventually involved the FASB and the IASC, as well as the Canadian and British standard-setters. Needless to say, they did not come up with identical standards, but IAS 21 was one of the outcomes of this process, and its cousins all use the same essential approach.

Originally IAS 21 offered two translation methods. Under the 'temporal method' you treat all the transactions of the subsidiary as though they had been carried out by the parent, and this means that all the exchange differences flow through the income statement. In particular the liabilities of the subsidiary will be translated at the closing rate (current rate at balance sheet date)

whereas the assets will be translated at the rates applicable when they were purchased.

The other method, which is now the only method used in IAS 21, is known as the 'net investment method'. It treats the subsidiary as though it were a stand-alone entity in which the parent had an investment. In that case the income statement is typically translated at the average rate for the year, and the balance sheet is translated at the closing rate. This has the merit of translating both the assets and the liabilities at the same rate, leaving the parent exposed to the foreign exchange risk only on the net asset position. Under IAS 21 the exchange difference on the net investment goes to a reserve line in equity, sometimes labelled the 'foreign currency translation adjustment'. The year on year change in this now goes to Other Comprehensive Income.

The key issue that determines which method is used is supposed to be the 'functional currency'. This is defined as 'the currency of the primary economic environment in which the subsidiary operates'. The standard elaborates that this is usually the one where the subsidiary generates and expends cash. It gives a number of factors to be considered, such as the currency that influences sale prices and costs, or in which it receives financing flows.

If the functional currency of the subsidiary is the same as that of the parent, the subsidiary is considered to be part of the foreign operations of the parent and the temporal method should be used. An example would be (say) the Norwegian subsidiary of a Swedish washing machine manufacturer. If the sales price in Norway is based on converting a Euro price, and the cost invoiced to Norway is also in Euros, one might well consider that the Norwegian subsidiary has the Euro as its functional currency.

If, however, the subsidiary's functional currency is not that of the parent, then the net investment method is used. In practice, it is extremely rare to see the temporal method used under IFRS. Many people think it distorts balance sheet relationships, and creates artificial volatility in the income statement.

A particular wrinkle of IAS 21 is that it also has the notion of a 'presentation currency'. This was not in the standard as originally written, but was added in 2003 when the IASB was carrying out a review of the standards it had inherited. Harry Schmid, formerly a senior accounting executive of Nestlé, was on the IASB at the time, as well as Tatsumi Yamada, a Japanese accountant. Traditionally consolidated financial statements are prepared in the currency of the parent.

However, the IASB took the point that sometimes the parent's currency is not the major trading currency of the group (Nestlé is based in Switzerland but transacts mostly in Euros and US dollars), or that the company is listed in major financial markets where most companies use a currency different from that of the reporting company. For example, some Japanese (and other) companies used to produce what were called 'convenience translations' where they simply took the parent company consolidated statements and translated them to US dollars at closing rate, which does not have any economic underpinning as a representation of the group.

Under IAS 21 then a company may opt to present its consolidated financial statements in a currency other than the parent's functional currency. This is called the presentation currency, and the translation methodology is then determined on whether the subsidiary's function currency is the same or different from the presentation currency.

Business combinations

IFRS 3 *Business Combinations* was, as its number suggests, one of the earliest standards issued by the IASB. It was an urgent priority whose object was to move IFRS into line with US GAAP. The FASB's SFAS 141 (issued in 2001) had significantly changed business combinations in the US by removing the possibility of merger accounting, or pooling of interests, and also doing away with the requirement to amortize goodwill.

Under merger accounting, the combination is done by an exchange of shares, but the shares of the issuing company are measured at nominal value and not market value, and the underlying assets and liabilities are not revalued. This sort of accounting was widely done in the US (for example, in the merger of Daimler and Chrysler). No goodwill was recognized and the actual value given up by one company to combine with the other was not easy to see. The FASB decided to put an end to such practices, but allowed that goodwill should not be amortized. Although analysts typically add back goodwill amortization, companies did not like having to amortize it as was required by US GAAP.

The IASB, of course, had a formal convergence programme with the FASB (agreed in 2002) but in any event wanted similarly to put an end to abusive merger accounting, and moved quickly to issue IFRS 3 *Business Combinations* in 2003, which converged closely with SFAS 141, and was subsequently revised when the FASB revised that standard. Aside from the apparent abuses of the merger approach, some standard-setters argued that while they could accept the notion of a merger of equals, there was no characteristic that was unique to a merger that would enable one to define a merger satisfactorily. Consequently all combinations would be treated as an acquisition by one company of another, and in all combinations an acquirer had to be identified.

The fundamental approach of IFRS 3, as with IAS 22 which it replaced, is that all the acquired assets and liabilities of a business must be recognized at fair value at the time of acquisition, and the net assets should be deducted from the purchase consideration to arrive at a goodwill figure. One difference not appreciated by constituents was that under IFRS 3 the consideration is the fair value given to the former owners, which does not include costs incurred by the acquiring entity.

The principle of fair value of acquired assets and liabilities is subject to exceptions specified in the standard, including leases, insurance contracts, deferred tax and pension liabilities. The assets and liabilities also have to be a business, and not just a bundle of assets. The principle does, however, extend to all identifiable assets and liabilities, irrespective of whether they were recognized in the acquired company's books. The

IFRS 3 definition of an identifiable asset says that it should be either (a) separable, or (b) arise from contractual or legal rights, even if these are not separable. Separable is defined as capable of being separated or transferred, individually or in combination with other assets and liabilities. This is a wider definition than was applied in some national GAAP, which typically required assets to be individually separable if they were to be recognized.

The (mandatory) application guidance notes that some assets will be subsumed into goodwill. It specifically mentions the assembled workforce in this category and the value of any contracts under negotiation at the time of the acquisition. The standard allows that some time will be needed to resolve all valuation and other issues connected with an acquisition. An entity has up to one year to finalize these, and must use estimates if necessary during that period.

The (mandatory) application guidance notes that some assets will be subsumed into goodwill

Once the goodwill has been measured, however, the acquirer needs to allocate it across cash generating units. Impairment comes under IAS 36, and is normally done at the level of the cash generating unit. The cash generating unit is the smallest group of assets that generates cash flows that are largely independent of cash inflows from other groups of assets. However, IAS 36 allows that goodwill should be pushed down only to the level at which it is monitored internally, with the proviso that this must be no higher than segment level. Goodwill can therefore be pushed down to a group of cash generating units for impairment purposes. When a cash generating unit is impaired, goodwill is the first asset to be written down, and goodwill impairment cannot be subsequently reversed.

IFRS 3 also has extensive disclosure requirements that are aimed at showing the allocation of consideration to the main classes of assets and liabilities, and also giving some basis for analysts to estimate the likely future impact of the acquisition on profits.

Investments in associates

If an investee company is not consolidated, i.e. the investor does not control it, there are currently a number of alternative treatments, some of which will disappear over time. The interest could be accounted for as an associate, or it may be a joint venture, or simply a financial instrument.

Having failed the control test, the next level of involvement recognized by IFRS is that of having 'significant influence'. IAS 28 *Investments in Associates* defines this as 'power to participate in the financial and operating policy decisions of the investee but is not control or joint control over those policies'. IAS 28 does not, though, apply to venture capital firms, mutual funds and similar professional investment vehicles. It does apply to joint ventures, as discussed below.

The standard suggests (IAS 28.7) several factors that would probably indicate that there is significant influence. One of these is representation on the board of directors of the investee, but others are any other participation in decision-making, the existence of significant transactions between investor and investee, interchange of management personnel and supply of necessary technology. The standard says also that significant influence is presumed to exist where the investor has 20% or more of the voting shares, and presumed not to exist where the shareholding is smaller (a carry through into IFRS of the US 'bright line' approach). It notes, however, that whether significant influence exists or not is a matter of judgement.

The equity method has long been used in consolidated accounts

If significant influence is presumed to exist, the investment is categorized as an 'associate' or associated company, and special measurement rules have to be followed. The investment must be accounted for using what is called the 'equity method'. The investor carries the investment at the proportion of the investee's net assets (or equity) applicable to the shareholding. A dividend received from the associate will write down the investment.

If there is a difference between the net asset value of the associate and the initial cost of the investment, any excess of cost over net asset value is treated as non-amortizable goodwill. Any excess of net assets is taken immediately to profit and loss.

The equity method has long been used in consolidated accounts (and also applied to individual company accounts). However, current standard-setters do not like it because they do not think it conveys useful information. On the positive side, it shows that the relationship is more than an arms-length investment where the return is dividends and eventual price appreciation. On the negative side, the book increase or decrease does not represent a current or possible future cash flow. In the longer run, people would like to fair value the investment, as this would give an approximation of what could be realized by selling the investment. This has not climbed to the top of the IASB's working list so far, and there are technical difficulties related to valuing unquoted investments, so a change to fair value accounting would likely meet pushback.

A new disclosure standard (IFRS 12) is due to be issued in 2011 but with an effective date of 2013 requires that entities discuss the basis on which they decided to treat significant investments as not being subsidiaries.

Joint ventures

IAS 31 *Interests in Joint Ventures* deals with joint ventures but a replacement standard (IFRS 11) is due to be issued in 2011. The replacement standard will probably have an effective date of 1 January 2013, with earlier adoption allowed. The new standard talks about 'joint arrangements' rather than joint ventures. As compared with IAS 31, the new standard prohibits the use of proportional consolidation, and bases the accounting on the substance of the arrangement rather than the legal form. Under IAS 31 where a joint venture was operated through a company in which the venturers each held shares, they would likely equity account their shareholding. If one venturer had a contract to manage the joint venture, that company would treat it as a subsidiary.

The analysis done by the initial project team, from the Australian standard-setter, was that some joint arrangements were more in the nature of pooling agreements where the venturers contributed assets and shared outputs. The new standard therefore says that the substance of the arrangement should determine the accounting. If the venturer has 'joint control' over an independent company, then it applies the equity method. However if it is contributing assets, or is responsible for liabilities, which are used in a joint arrangement but which remain under its ownership, these should be accounted for using the appropriate asset or liability standard. These would be treated as an 'investment in joint operations' in the balance sheet.

Assets held for disposal

This subject is dealt with at more length in Chapter 6, but it is appropriate to mention it here as well. IFRS 5 *Non-current assets Held for Sale and Discontinued Operations* provides broadly that where a company has decided to dispose of an asset, it should thereafter be classified in the balance sheet as an asset held for disposal. Its results should be similarly disclosed separately in the profit and loss account (income statement). This frequently affects investments in other companies. On the one hand, large groups 'churn' their activities fairly regularly, getting rid of operations that are no longer sufficiently profitable, or no longer fit strategy. Once the decision has been taken to sell a subsidiary, all its assets and liabilities are classified separately and should be measured at fair value less selling costs.

The other fairly frequently occurring case is where a company takes over another group, but decides to sell one or more subsidiaries immediately, either in response to regulatory specifications or because they do not fit the enlarged group. In such a case the operations that are being sold are removed from the purchase price allocation as a disposal group and are accounted for as such until sale.

Equity investments

If an equity investment is not accounted for as a subsidiary, nor as an associate, and not as a joint arrangement, and it is not being held for disposal, then it is a financial instrument. Here too the financial arrangements are in the middle of change. IAS 39, which deals with the accounting for financial instruments, is being progressively replaced by IFRS 9, which has an effective date of 1 January 2013 (with earlier adoption possible).

Under IAS 39 all equity investments in shares that are listed on a stock exchange are valued at fair value, with changes in fair value going through profit and loss. However, shares that are not quoted on a stock market can be accounted for at historical cost, with dividends going to profit and loss. This exception has been removed by IFRS 9, which specifies that all equity investments must be at fair value.

There was a good deal of opposition to this requirement because it was pointed out that estimating fair values was extremely difficult in any but the most developed markets because of the absence of transactions. The IASB refused to give way on the principle but added application guidance as follows:

in limited circumstances, cost may be an appropriate estimate of fair value. That may be the case if insufficient more recent information is available to determine fair value, or if there is a wide range of possible fair value measurements and cost represents the best estimate of fair value within that range.

(IFRS 9, Appendix B paragraph B5.5)

The fairly clear implication is that cost may well be a reasonable approximation of fair value, subject to the test that one should estimate fair value and be prepared to show that cost comes inside the range of possible fair values.

IFRS 9 has a further element: where a company has an equity investment that it deems to be 'strategic', this may be measured at fair value, but fair value changes will flow through Other Comprehensive Income. A company wanting to use this option has to make an irrevocable choice on first accounting for the investment. This exception appears to have been given for Japanese companies. Large groups there typically have multiple cross-holdings with each other, rather than the US control pyramid. The shareholdings are held indefinitely, and it is argued that the possible changes in value of the shares are irrelevant as they are held as part of a business and trading arrangement.

disclosure of investor/investee relationships and accounting decisions is set to become more elaborate

Conclusion

As noted at the beginning of this chapter, general purpose financial statements under IFRS must include all the businesses with which the reporting entity has a relationship. The different kinds of investor/investee relationship that are possible are addressed by a multiplicity of different accounting arrangements. The central issue is that all assets and liabilities that are controlled by the entity should be reported, irrespective of ownership. The most important central issue is identifying what investee entities should be fully consolidated.

This area is undergoing considerable change, but the most significant of these affect joint arrangements and financial instruments where there is no control. However, disclosure of investor/investee relationships and accounting decisions is set to become more elaborate.

Appendix: Fair value measurement

Fair value has been used for very many years as a means of fixing an accounting value where there is none. As we saw in this chapter, the acquisition of another company requires the integration of a bundle of assets and liabilities into the consolidated accounts. You don't have individual values for these, only a figure for the whole bundle. Fair value is then used as an allocation device to break down the total price into the components. Similarly, if you do a barter transaction, referring to market price enables you to find an accounting value. If you exchange your car and pay €5,000 for another car, the market value of the car you exchanged will enable you to derive an accounting value for the car acquired.

The use of fair value is, of itself, not necessarily controversial. It causes problems with financial instruments because their market value fluctuates and people do not like importing volatility into their balance sheets. At a theoretical level you could measure all assets and liabilities at fair value. If you did this, every company's balance sheet would be directly comparable, and the data would give you the market's estimate of the cash generating potential of the company (if you subscribe to the view strongly held by the finance community that the market price of anything – in a perfect and efficient market – reflects the market's valuation of the expected future benefits of owning that asset). If the objective of financial reporting, as the IASB conceptual framework says, is to provide information about future cash flows, fair value would seem to do the trick! However, in the real world markets are never perfect, and often there is no observable fair value, so the theoretical ideal is not achievable. People have widely differing views as to how useful an estimated or approximate fair value might be.

Fair value measurement has been, and remains, a controversial subject, therefore, for standard-setters. Much of the controversy, however, is related to its use for measuring financial instruments, mostly therefore in the financial statements of banks or insurance companies. We will not look at that here – that pleasure will come later. In this section we will just address the ground rules for **how** you measure under fair value, and not **when** or **whether** you should measure at fair value.

The IASB aims to issue a standard on fair value measurement in 2011. Its aim is to align the IFRS literature with that of the US and its Accounting Standards Codification Topic 820. The main lines are that fair value is an exit price – what you would get for **selling** an asset in the market to which you have access (or what you would have to pay to transfer a liability). Fair value is always a measurement derived from a market participant's view, and is not derived from the company's own view. For example, if using fair value to allocate the acquisition cost of a bundle of assets and liabilities, the price is what a market participant would pay, and does not reflect the intentions of the acquiring company. If you acquire a factory in order to close it down and transfer production elsewhere, that is not a consideration.

The market

Historically the term 'fair value' has been used in the courts and in contracts in the US and UK, and probably in other anglophone legal systems, to mean a price at which both buyer and seller are equally satisfied. The modern US accounting standard has, however, defined it as a selling price for measurement purposes. A conundrum that perturbs people is that the US standard says that buying price and selling price are the same in the same market. People find this counter-intuitive, because you cannot generally sell something for the price at which you bought it. The explanation is that if you immediately wanted to sell the good, you are changing markets.

This is more easily understood with an example, and we will take one beloved of the IASB: if you buy a brand new BMW from a dealer for €50,000, your buying price is the same as the dealer's selling price, by definition. In the dealer market, entry and exit price are the same in that sense. However, if you decide to sell immediately, you are not a BMW dealer, you cannot sell in that market. You must sell in the second-hand car market, where people will demand a discount from the dealer's price to compensate for the fact that they have no choice of colour, accessories, engine, etc., which they could have from the dealer. If the same person switches from buyer to seller, they are also switching markets, and the price at which they can buy is usually different from the price at which they can sell.

The forthcoming IFRS require that the market price used is that which could be obtained in 'the most advantageous market', but adding that this should be the market the company normally uses. The fair value is also less the costs of getting the asset to the market. In other words if the best price for corn is to be had in Chicago, but your corn is in East Africa, you do not normally take the Chicago price, and if you did, you would have to adjust for transport.

Measurement hierarchy

The standard accepts that while in some cases it may be easy to find a market price, in others it may not. It therefore uses a three-level hierarchy in order to distinguish different levels of closeness to the market and to communicate uncertainty in the measurement through that. The most desirable level of fair value measurement is Level 1 where you are able to see transactions for exactly the same asset taking place in a liquid market: you have an 'observable' input that is an exact match. The second most desirable is Level 2, where you still have observable inputs, transactions in a liquid market, but the assets are not exactly the same. An example of this would be that you want to measure at fair value a three-bedroom apartment in a block where only two-bedroom apartments are currently being traded. You could make a Level 2 measurement by taking a current two-bedroom apartment and adjusting upwards for the extra bedroom. You cannot prove that the selling price is correct, but it is anchored on another price and should not be too far out.

Finally you come to Level 3, which is entirely an estimate, based on unobservable inputs. You use Level 3 when there is no market, or the market is illiquid (such as during the financial crisis) and you estimate the fair value by modelling an exit transaction. Some people refer to this as 'mark to model', whereas Levels 1 and 2 are called 'mark to market'. The model used can be any reasonably respectable model, and indeed you are encouraged to use more than one model in order to satisfy yourself that you are not choosing a model that gives you a result that is an outlier. Auditors will certainly be happier if you can back up the estimate with similar figures from several models.

To take the apartment pricing example above, another way to value the apartment would be to estimate the rental net of costs that could be earned and multiply that by a factor used by the investment property business. So, say an estimated net rental of €18,000 a year multiplied by 15 (industry payback period) would give you a selling price of €270,000.

Does it matter which level of fair value you use? Well, research says it does. You have to disclose the nature of your fair values, and if you use Level 3 you have to disclose details of your assumptions, the sensitivity of the estimate to key variables, etc. Research says investors discount Level 3 valuations fairly substantially, which makes listed company CFOs reluctant to use them.

Highest and best use

Another potential hazard in the fair value approach of the IASB and FASB is that fair value must be based on the highest and best use (although this is restricted to non-financial assets). Some people argue that this adds another very subjective dimension to valuation. Does the company necessarily know what the market thinks is the highest and best use? Clearly there is a role for judgement here. The fundamental idea is that the market value should give some idea of whether the company is making an adequate return on the assets under its control. If the asset is not being put to its best use, this information should be available to investors. It is not clear how realistic an expectation this is.

Linked to this is the notion that the approach to fair value could be 'in use' or 'in exchange'. This is an important subtlety that is not much discussed in the literature. Fair value is **not necessarily** a selling price in all circumstances. An 'in exchange' fair value for an asset is the selling price on the market. However, the 'in use' premise is relevant when an asset might not be capable of generating cash flows on its own, but would always be associated with other assets and liabilities in a group that together generate cash flows (a 'cash generating unit'). In this case the assumption must be that a market participant would have access to a similar bundle of assets and liabilities, and the appropriate valuation is the replacement cost of the individual asset.

Liabilities

The fair value of a liability is the amount that a market participant would require to take over responsibility for the liability (but it is not the amount to **settle** the liability – the assumption is that the liability will remain outstanding until the normal settlement date). The standard acknowledges that there is rarely a market for liabilities, and says that in the first instance one should look at the market for the asset that is the other side of the liability (your liability is your creditor's asset). If there is an active market for the asset, then this price should be used in line with the Level 1 and Level 2 approaches. If there is no observable market, then a Level 3 approach is necessary.

A Level 3 approach includes estimating the likely cash outflows, but also allowing for uncertainties in the cash flows and adjusting for the time value of money. The standard also says that a market participant would require compensation for assuming the risk (risk premium). This is one reason why there will be a significant difference between the entity's own valuation of the settlement value and that of a market participant. The standard also requires that the valuation take account of 'non-performance risk'. This includes the credit risk of the instrument. Here again, many constituents are uncomfortable with this.

They regard it as giving counter-intuitive results – an increase in credit risk reduces the value of the liability.

Conclusion

The new standard sets out the detailed rules for measuring something at 'pure' fair value. However, it does not say under what circumstances fair value should be used – that is to be found in other standards. In those other standards you will also often find restrictions on the use of fair value. So in IFRS 5 *Non-current Assets Held for Sale*, the valuation rule is fair value less costs to sell. Basically fair value is a market selling price, and reflects the assumptions that a knowledgeable market participant would make.

CHAPTER 4

INCOME STATEMENT ITEMS

This chapter looks at a series of standards that primarily impact items in the income statement. It starts with the revenue recognition standards, including customer loyalty schemes and onerous contracts and discusses the forthcoming revenue recognition joint standard. It also addresses agriculture, government grants and pensions, as well as stock options, inventories, income tax, interest and foreign exchange differences.

The actual presentation of the income statement or profit and loss account is to be found in Chapter 2. In this chapter we will look at the various standards that have an impact on the recognition and measurement of items that are reported in the income statement. Of course many things that affect the income statement will also affect the balance sheet and vice versa, so the split of subjects between this chapter and the next one on the balance sheet is to some extent subjective.

Revenue recognition

To start with the top line, IAS 18 *Revenue* is the basic standard that determines the sales number, and excludes from its scope revenue recognition that is dealt with in specific standards such as IFRS 9 *Financial Instruments*, IAS 17 *Leases* and IAS 41 *Agriculture*. The standard defines as revenue anything that increases an entity's assets or decreases its liabilities. It says that: 'Revenue is recognized when it is probable that future economic benefits will flow to the entity and these benefits can be measured reliably'.

This principle is expanded to note that revenue is recognized when the entity has transferred to the buyer the significant risks and rewards of ownership of the goods. The entity must have neither 'continuing managerial involvement' nor control of the goods. When the sale relates to the provision of services, the standard specifies that revenue is recognized in relation to a stage of completion of a contract. This is subject to being able to identify such a stage reliably, costs being identified reliably and measurable future benefits being likely. Construction contracts are dealt with in a separate standard, discussed below.

The basic approach on measurement is that the transaction should be measured at fair value, and the standard specifies that this is normally the value of the consideration received. However, it cannot be assumed that the consideration is always fair value. One particular case where the consideration is not the transaction price is where extended credit is given. For example, where a car manufacturer sells a car for €18,000 with three years' credit at zero interest rate and monthly payments of €500, the transaction price will be the present value of instalment payments at whatever is the current rate for car finance. If the appropriate discount rate were 8%, this would give a present value of €14,200. The car manufacturer would book the transaction as a sale at €14,200 and the balance of €3,800 would be recognized as interest income over the three years, calculated according to the balance outstanding.

A further detail here concerns customer loyalty schemes. The appendix to IAS 18 allows two possibilities for accounting for these, either by allocating the revenue or by recognizing a liability. A 2007 Interpretation, IFRIC 13 *Customer Loyalty Programmes*, rules, however, that where a customer loyalty scheme results in a customer receiving the right to some further asset or service when they carry out a transaction, the consideration for the original transaction has to be allocated over both elements. The entity has to allocate the original revenue in proportion to the fair value of the first transaction and the fair value of the reward transaction.

> *The basic approach on measurement is that the transaction should be measured at fair value*

This latter is based on the value of the award and the likelihood of someone claiming it. To take an example, if a sack of dog biscuits costs €50 and the supplier offers a voucher for 20% off the next purchase, the nominal value of the reward is €10 (20% of €50) and likelihood of it being claimed is 50%, this gives a fair value of €5. So the revenue on the initial purchase is recognized as (€50 * 50/55=) €45.45 and the deferred revenue carried forward is (€5 * 5/55=) €4.55.

This treatment should be compared with the accounting for guarantees and indemnities. These fall under IAS 37 *Provisions, Contingent Liabilities and Contingent Assets*, which mandates recognition of a liability based on what it would cost the entity to transfer the liability to another entity. Consequently under a guarantee arrangement, the initial transaction gives rise to full recognition of the consideration as immediate revenue, while any residual guarantee is expensed as a liability.

IAS 18 has an appendix of illustrative examples. These address a number of particular kinds of sale transaction such as those where acceptance of the goods is subject to installation and delivery – revenue is recognized by the supplier when the client accepts the goods, and not when they are delivered. Against that, bill and hold arrangements where the client acquires title, but delivery is delayed with the client's agreement, result in revenue being recognized when the goods are available. Subscription sales paid in advance have to be recognized on a straight line basis over the life of the subscription.

Barter transactions are measured at the fair value of the goods or services exchanged. However there is a 2001 Interpretation (SIC 31 *Revenue – Barter Transactions Involving Advertising*) that attempts to address abuses that became common during the internet bubble where two entities swap advertising and put massive revenue through their profit and loss account. The net effect on profit is nil, but gives the impression of high activity rates. The Interpretation says the swap must be calibrated against other sales of the same advertising for cash.

IAS 11 *Construction Contracts* is the other main standard addressing revenue recognition. The objective of the standard is 'the allocation of contract revenue and contract costs to the accounting periods in which construction work is performed'. The standard specifies that this must be followed by construction companies. In other words, accounting for contracts only on completion, which is a favourite approach when aiming to defer taxation, is not allowed. The standard allows that several related contracts may be treated as one for accounting purposes, or a single contract with different clearly definable elements could be treated as several contracts.

The standard requires that when the outcome of the contract can be estimated reliably, revenue should be recognized in respect of each stage of the contract. This should be done using the percentage of completion method – revenue is recognized in the same proportion as the costs incurred to date bear to total expected costs. The costs to be considered are all costs directly attributable to the contract, and indirect costs such as depreciation of equipment used in the construction, construction overheads, design costs, insurance but not including general administration costs or selling costs.

Onerous contracts are addressed under IAS 37. This requires that where the estimated costs to fulfilment of the contract are higher than the expected revenue, the difference should be recognized immediately in profit and loss.

You should be aware that the IASB and FASB issued a joint exposure draft on Revenue Recognition in June 2010. The project plan calls for a final standard to be voted on by June 2011 but no expected application date has been published. July 2013 would be the earliest possible date and 2015 is more likely, with early adoption permitted, which may be useful to countries moving to IFRS in 2011.

In headline terms, the new proposals will change practice very little. The main area that they will impact is contracts with multiple deliverables (such as construction contracts). The exposure draft says that revenue is recognized when control of an asset passes to the client. This does not fit very well with IAS 11, since in many construction contracts, and above all in turnkey operations, the client does not take control of anything until the end of the contract. The draft suggests that such contracts should be segmented and where the contract is for a supply of a series of construction services, these are in effect passed to the customer where delivered. In other words, the contract should not be for an asset but for the supply of the goods and services necessary to construct the asset.

The main innovation of the proposal is that it calls for recognition of a contract asset when the entity has a non-cancellable contract, and a contract performance obligation to fulfil that contract. The net impact on the balance sheet will be zero, because the proposal is that the performance obligation will be measured at the value of the contract asset (unless it is an onerous contract at inception, which ought to be rare) and the two will be offset. It does, though, represent an advance in information about the company since contracts on which work has not started ('executory contracts') are not reported under IFRS at present. In effect this method provides information about the order book.

The standard-setters say that the idea of the proposal is to provide a single authoritative source for revenue recognition that will provide comparable information for all revenue recognition questions. They say it will enhance consistency. In the US there are many industry-specific standards that address such issues, and the FASB hopes to replace these with this unified approach.

Agriculture

International standards include hardly any industry-specific guidelines, as compared with many individual countries. A major exception concerns agriculture, which is dealt with in IAS 41 *Agriculture*. This standard was written at the behest of the World Bank, which gave the International Accounting Standards Committee (IASC – the original body that became the IASB in 2001) a significant grant to provide it. Even so the subject kept getting deferred from the agenda and it was to be the very last standard issued by the IASC.

International standards include hardly any industry-specific guidelines

Broadly the standard aims to measure agricultural revenue in the year when the increase in value took place, rather than only on sale of the assets. In that sense it is very similar to IAS 11 *Construction Contracts* – revenue is measured as earned and not deferred until the completion of the transaction. Unlike IAS 11, the agriculture standard calls on agricultural entities to measure their livestock and other living assets ('biological assets') at fair value less costs to sell at each reporting date. IAS 41 is therefore the nearest thing there is in IFRS to a 'full fair value' approach to accounting, even though it falls slightly short because it mandates the deduction of selling costs.

However, it also does not necessarily fit fair value as now defined because where there is no active market, value must be estimated as a proportion of the likely sales proceeds when the asset would be sold. To give an example, if a farmer plants a field of poplar trees that will be ready for harvest in 10 years, the farmer would be very unlikely to be able to sell one-year-old saplings. The wood has no value until it reaches maturity, and so the value is estimated by calculating its sale price at maturity, discounting this for uncertainties and allocating this across the growing period. Against that, there is a market for calves, which farmers with available pasture may buy in order to keep them while they grow to full maturity. Consequently there are market prices available at different points in the production cycle.

Government grants

In agriculture, as well as other areas, government grants may well be an important form of revenue. IAS 20 *Accounting for Government Grants and Disclosure of Government Assistance* specifies that government grants should be released to the profit and loss account systematically over the periods meant to benefit from them. Where the grant is a revenue grant, meant to compensate for costs incurred by the business, the grant is recognized in the income statement at the same time as the related costs. Where the government gives a grant to subsidize the purchase of an asset, the standard allows two treatments. Either the grant is set up as a deferred credit and is released over the same period as the related asset is depreciated, or the grant is offset directly against the asset, thereby reducing the depreciation charge directly.

Sometimes grants are given on a contingent basis – they have to be paid back if the recipient fails to carry out some promised activity. In this case the standard says that grant is recognized when there is reasonable assurance that the entity will comply with the conditions. In a similar way, government support is sometimes given through loans that may be at an artificially low interest rate, or may eventually be forgiven. Where the interest rate is subsidized, the difference between that and a commercial rate has to be recognized as a government grant. A forgivable loan is recognized as a grant when it becomes reasonably certain that the conditions will be met. The standard includes a disclosure package.

Some members of the IASB regard IAS 20 as typical of a 'smoothing' approach, where emphasis is given to maintaining a steady earnings flow as opposed to measuring changes in assets and liabilities. On top of that IAS 20 allows a choice in how you present a grant related to an asset, with the result that there will be a loss of comparability between similar entities. Someone who buys the asset without a grant will show different values to the person who has a grant and offsets it against the asset, which will also distort measures such as return on capital employed. A pure 'asset and liability' person would say that a deferred credit is not an asset, it is a direct transfer of wealth from the government to the entity and should be shown as immediate income.

Notwithstanding the distaste of the asset and liability enthusiasts on the IASB, during its first decade the standard has not been put on the active agenda for revision. Their programme has been too pressured by more immediate challenges such as getting ready for EU adoption in 2005 and more recently resolving financial crisis accounting issues. However, its smoothing approach contrasts strongly with the quasi-fair value approach of the agriculture standard, written 20 years later.

Pensions

In countries where significant pensions are often provided by employers, accounting for company-funded pension schemes is a contentious subject. It has been targeted by the SEC as an area where many corporate liabilities remain off balance sheet. The most difficult area is the 'defined benefit' pension scheme where the employer promises to pay a pension that is calculated on the employee's salary at the time they retire. In order to calculate the cost of providing the pension to be expensed proportionately as the employee delivers service to the entity, it is necessary to estimate the employee's likely final salary, likely period from retirement to death, and the likely return on assets that would meet the pension requirements over that time. Clearly the margin for error is considerable, and as life expectancy has grown, the need to make catch-up adjustments has been considerable.

Many companies set up such schemes years ago when employees often died a year or two after retirement, but employers now find themselves paying pensions for people who are living 20 to 30 years after retirement. As a consequence many such schemes are being run down, but they remain a problem, particularly in mature companies where profitability may be declining while the number of retired staff still on the books is growing. There are companies where the value of the pension scheme is greater than the market value of the company.

The IASB standard that covers pension costs is IAS 19 *Employee Benefits*, which was first issued in 1982. This deals with pension schemes and any other benefits, such as health care, that are provided to retired staff. The main objective is to recognize the costs of providing post-employment benefits during the accounting periods when the employee is working for the entity. IAS 19, like many IFRS, is in a state of transition. The IASB proposes to amend the standard in the near future to address some immediate problems (likely effective date 2012) while also intending to do a thorough review of the whole issue thereafter, possibly in conjunction with the US. If that review is done, it would be unlikely to result in any changes before 2020.

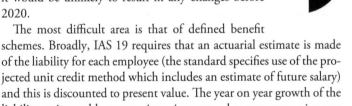

There are companies where the value of the pension scheme is greater than the market value of the company

The most difficult area is that of defined benefit schemes. Broadly, IAS 19 requires that an actuarial estimate is made of the liability for each employee (the standard specifies use of the projected unit credit method which includes an estimate of future salary) and this is discounted to present value. The year on year growth of the liability, using stable assumptions, is expensed as current service cost in the profit and loss account.

However, where the assumptions change, most often because of changes in actual experience such as longer life expectancy, there is an actuarial loss. Under IAS 19 in force in 2010, such a loss can be taken to profit and loss, it can be recognized in Other Comprehensive Income, or it can be deferred, or it can be ignored under the 'corridor' method. Basically the corridor method specifies that a change of less than 10% can be ignored. If the change is more than 10%, then it can be amortized over the remaining service life of the employees. One of the changes proposed in the exposure draft to amend IAS 19 published in April 2010 is the removal of the corridor deferral system in favour of immediate recognition in Other Comprehensive Income or profit and loss. The liability for pensions, under IAS 19 known as the 'Defined Benefit Obligation', will be shown as a liability in the balance sheet.

Defined benefit schemes are usually, but by no means always, funded by the employer. Typically the employer constitutes a fund of assets that are separate from the employer company in the event of bankruptcy and which are dedicated to meeting payments to retired staff. The difference between this fund and the pension liability is usually referred to as the 'pension deficit' or 'pension surplus', as the case may be. The Defined Benefit Obligation is reduced by the plan assets, which are valued at fair value. As you would expect, the use of fair value means that the asset value fluctuates from year to year, providing another gain or loss to go in the actuarial gains and losses line for the pension plan.

A further complication is that the entity takes to profit and loss the expected return on plan assets, with the difference between this and the actual return forming part of the fair value change. Under the proposed changes to IAS 19, the service cost would appear in the profit and loss account as an employment cost, the actual return on plan assets would go to interest income, and the actuarial gains and losses would most likely go to Other Comprehensive Income.

The other main type of pension scheme is the Defined Contribution Scheme, where the employer (and potentially the employee) pay into a fund – rather like a life insurance policy – and the employee receives a pension based on the amount of money in the fund at retirement.

Since the employer has no responsibility for the outcome, the only accounting issue is expensing the employer's contribution on a period by period basis.

Another kind of arrangement that may be found is the multi-employer scheme. Insurance companies and other financial institutions sometimes organize free-standing schemes in which any number of employers can participate. Even when these schemes are defined benefit, the employer expenses all of the contribution made each year and no pension liability appears on the employer's balance sheet.

The standard also addresses other unpaid employee benefits such as leave and sickness benefit. While an employee is still in service, an accrual should be made for accumulated leave entitlement that has not been used, and any other short-term benefit. For long-term benefits a liability should be estimated and its present value recognized, without use of the corridor.

There are extensive disclosures required about pension plans and a multinational employer with plans in several countries may well find they have to provide several pages of notes. Disclosures include the changes in the defined benefit obligation and fair value of plan assets. The notes should provide the discount rate used to arrive at the present value of the obligation as well as main assumptions and should provide some detail on the way in which the pension fund is invested.

Stock options

Another subject that was particularly controversial in the 1990s was the practice, very common in certain industries, of rewarding management by giving them options to buy shares at interesting prices in exchange for meeting targets or staying with the employer through a difficult period, etc. One of the reasons for the attractiveness of this payment method was that there was no impact on the income statement. The shares were issued when they had vested (i.e. the employee had fulfilled the conditions) and the employee wanted to exercise the option. This transaction appeared as a sale of equity and was mentioned only in the analysis of changes in equity.

Companies argued that this was a transaction between equity holders and management and not between the company and management, and therefore there was no reason to recognize an expense. Standard-setters argued that issuing equity was no different from paying cash – the recipient received an asset that gave them future benefits – so the issue of the equity was an expense. The FASB had had difficulties with this area in the 1990s and when the IASB started work in 2001 it decided that issuing an international standard would be a demonstration of the utility of having an international standard-setter. Where national standard-setters faced the argument that they were putting their national companies at a competitive disadvantage if they took the initiative, the IASB could show leadership without these constraints.

Consequently the IASB issued IFRS 2 *Share-based Payment* in 2003.

The essence of this standard is that any transaction by a company where it acquires goods and services in exchange for shares, or an option to buy shares, calls for an expense to be recognized. While the principle is clear and simple, the application is more complex! The difficulty arises in knowing how to measure the transaction.

Standard-setters argued that issuing equity was no different from paying cash

The standard addresses all transactions involving the exchange of shares for goods or services, but its widespread use occurs only in relation to the issue of share options to employees. The typical transaction involves three stages: (1) the agreement between company and employee on the terms of the option – known as 'grant date'; (2) the moment when the employee has fulfilled the conditions and can thereafter claim the shares – known as 'vesting date'; and (3) the date when the employee actually buys the shares – known as 'exercise date'.

The measurement problem is not unlike that found in pensions and other issues – you need to determine the amount of an expense for a period which is some time, maybe years, before the actual amount of the expense becomes known. In this case the transaction crystallizes when the employee exercises the option, but this is necessarily after the option vests and after the grant date. However, the expense should normally fall in the period between grant date and vesting date.

The solution is based on a formula that the FASB had partially introduced into the US in the 1990s. The company must estimate the fair value of the option at grant date and then allocate that over the period during which services are being provided to the company. However, the fair value has usually to be calculated by taking the market value, adjusting for volatility of the share price over the period and other issues such as the non-transferability of the option. This fair value per share must then be multiplied by the number of employees expected to remain with the company until vesting date. In a scheme involving a number of employees, this will usually be less than the total number of employees entering the scheme. Over the life of the option, the company must re-estimate the figures for numbers vesting in the light of the actual experience, but the fair value of the option remains fixed at the time as at grant date. The rationale is that the company entered into a contract at grant date; both company and employee had some sense of the value of the contract. The accounting reflects that arrangement, irrespective of what the ultimate exercise price might be.

This standard has proved to be quite troublesome in its application, because the detail of many arrangements can be different from the model presumed in the original standard. For example, an employee in a subsidiary might be granted stock options on the shares of the parent. There are also specific national statutory arrangements for putting profits aside into a fund to buy shares for employees, savings schemes that turn into shares, etc. On top of the different kinds of scheme there are also problems about what happens if an employee drops out but retains some rights, or the terms of the scheme are changed before the scheme has run its full course. The standard has been the subject of a number of clarifying amendments since it was issued.

Inventories

This is an area that obviously impacts both income statement and statement of financial position (balance sheet), but we will address it within the income statement chapter. IAS 2 *Inventories*, as its number implies, is a venerable standard that was first issued in 1975, even if it has been revised extensively in 1993 and was also reviewed in the IASB's 2003 improvements to their inherited standards, when some options were removed. The standard does not apply to agricultural products or construction contracts measured under IAS 11, nor does it apply to commodity brokers who measure inventories at fair value less costs to sell.

The standard specifies that inventories are held at the lower of cost or net realizable value

The standard specifies that inventories are held at the lower of cost or net realizable value. The standard goes into some detail as to what costs should be incorporated into the carrying value of inventory, and this is sometimes analogized to in other areas where costs are capitalized. Where costs have to be allocated to individual units by a formula, the standard mandates only First In First Out (FIFO) and weighted average. Last in First Out (LIFO) is not permitted, which might be a problem for US companies if they adopted IFRS, as it is allowed for tax purposes in the US.

Net realizable value is defined as the estimated selling price in the ordinary course of business less the estimated costs of completion and the estimated costs necessary to make the sale. Write-downs to net realizable value should be taken to income in the period when the write-down is made. They should also be reviewed subsequently.

The standard mandates disclosure in the notes of amounts of inventory expensed in the period and write-downs as well as the total carrying amount, split down into classifications relevant to the business.

Income taxes

Taxes represent an important cash outflow for businesses, and as a consequence many businesses try to manage their transactions and their accounting in such a way as will defer payment of taxation for as long as possible. This is, however, not consistent with accruals accounting generally and the IFRS approach of preparing financial statements that are representationally faithful to the state of the business.

As a consequence accruals-style adjustments (deferred taxation) have to be made to ensure that the consolidated financial statements reflect the tax that would have to be paid on the transactions reported, rather than reflecting only the tax actually paid. It is a normal arrangement in multinational companies that the individual financial statements of subsidiaries are drawn up to maximize national tax advantage, but these are adjusted for input to the consolidated statements drawn up under IFRS.

IAS 12 *Income Taxes* addresses what can be a very complex issue for multinational companies. It is based on an asset and liability approach to deferred taxation, as opposed to a transactional approach. It says that the company must address the future tax implications of the recovery of an asset or settlement of a liability in the balance sheet (statement of financial position) at reporting date.

An obvious cause of difference is when the entity recognizes unrealized losses and gains in the financial statements that will not be considered for tax purposes until the transaction is realized. For example, when you recognize a fair value gain on an equity investment, there will be no immediate tax payment, but you will have to pay tax when you finally sell the equity. IAS 12 says that in that case, if the appropriate tax on such a gain is 30% and you make an unrealized gain of €10m, you should make a provision for deferred tax of €3m.

Consequently the income statement will show a gain of €10m less tax of €3m, and the balance sheet will show a deferred tax liability of €3m. Similarly, if you make an impairment provision against property, you are anticipating a loss that would when realized reduce your actual tax. So an impairment provision of €5m would be offset by a deferred tax credit of €1.5m and a deferred tax asset for the same amount.

the IFRS has to stand above national law

The IASB has made several attempts to simplify IAS 12 and also to converge it more with US GAAP. As the standard-setters used to joke, the US and international standards have exactly the same fundamental approach – but make different exceptions, so do not produce the same result. However, the US standard is consistent with US tax law, whereas the IFRS has to stand above national law, so many years of trying to improve the standard were abandoned in 2009 when the IASB decided to give up trying to converge the tax standards.

This does not, of course, mean that there will not be changes to IAS 12! The IASB is planning to address one or two issues in the standard considered by constituents to need change as soon as possible. A longer term review of taxation is certainly possible but the standard-setters would have to be convinced that there is the possibility of a simpler standard.

Interest expense

IAS 23 *Borrowing Costs* is another of the standards that gives the IASB more trouble than the subject would seem to merit. While generally it requires interest incurred to be expensed, the main area of contention is what to do with any interest cost that is incurred during the construction of a non-current asset. In theory, the book value of an asset is all of the costs incurred to bring it into service, and where an entity borrows money to build an asset, the cost of borrowing is part of the cost of the asset, up to the point it enters service.

As originally written, IAS 23 left a choice; you could either expense the interest as incurred or you could capitalize into the cost of the asset. Most people tended to choose expensing because that is the most efficient from a tax perspective. If you expense the interest, it is immediately deductible, whereas if you roll it up into the book value of the asset, it is only deducted through depreciation over a number of years.

However, US GAAP requires that the interest is capitalized into an asset under construction. Consequently the IASB decided to remove the expensing option as part of its convergence programme. This means that, if you are a continental European country where the interest has to be in the accounts as an expense to be deducted, you would need to expense it in a subsidiary using local GAAP to get the tax benefit and then re-state for IFRS consolidated accounts. Evidently it is a disincentive to using IFRS for individual subsidiaries, without normally being a frequently occurring item, or major when it does occur.

One of the criticisms that people make of this standard is that it was changed to require capitalization of interest on assets under construction in the interests of convergence, but the change did not touch the other major issue related to this, which is how you identify the finance used for the project and what interest rate you assume. In very few cases can a company point to a specific loan for a specific project, so there the entity has to make allocations. The approach to these is different as between the US GAAP and IASB solutions, so convergence has been only half achieved.

IAS 23 requires entities to capitalize borrowing costs for a 'qualifying asset'. This is defined as an asset that takes a substantial amount of time to be made ready for use. It excludes assets that are bought in a condition where they can be used immediately. Inventory could count as a qualifying asset if it takes a substantial amount of time to be manufactured, but this excludes inventory that is 'routinely manufactured' or produced on a regular basis over a short period of time. If there is borrowing directly related to the project, this is capitalized, but where this is not the case, the company must capitalize a proportion of the weighted cost of its overall borrowings.

Foreign exchange differences

Leaving aside the question of translating the financial statements of subsidiaries that use a different currency (discussed in Chapter 3), we need to look at foreign exchange differences arising on transactions, and for simplicity we will also deal with differences on outstanding assets and liabilities denominated in a foreign currency.

IAS 21 *The Effects of Changes in Foreign Exchange Rates* says that an item denominated in a foreign currency will be recognized at the point where IFRS would require recognition, and will be measured by conversion at the spot rate to the company's operating currency ('functional currency' – the one in which it primarily transacts). If the transaction is for cash, that is the end of the matter; however, if the transaction is on credit, subsequent settlement of the outstanding receivable or payable will likely give rise to a foreign exchange gain or loss. This is recognized as a foreign exchange item in the profit and loss account and does not impact the measurement of the original transaction.

As originally written, IAS 21 also dealt with hedges of individual transactions, but this was removed subsequently and the standard now refers entities to IAS 39 *Financial Instrument: Recognition and Measurement.* Broadly the hedging instrument is measured at fair value at each reporting date, with gains and losses on the hedging instrument taken to Other Comprehensive Income (OCI). When the hedged item matures, the net gain or loss on the hedging instrument is 'recycled' from OCI to profit and loss. That is to say the net result is reversed out of OCI and transferred to current profit and loss.

As a general rule, financial assets and liabilities that are denominated in a foreign currency (i.e. not in the functional currency) have to be re-measured at each reporting date using the spot rate applicable at that date. The gains and losses are taken to profit and loss. Some people feel that re-measuring these assets and liabilities is not useful, since all that 'matters' is the final gain or loss when the asset or liability is settled. If you analogized with plant, for example, very often manufacturing plant has a very low salvage value, but you do not reduce its book value on that basis. The counter argument is that while you would have no interest in selling your plant, you could conceivably trade financial assets or settle liabilities or enter into a foreign currency hedge. Also it is argued that the spot rate for a currency impounds everything that the market knows about the future at that time, and is therefore the best predictor of settlement value.

Accounting in hyperinflationary economies

For completeness, we should mention that IFRS include a standard on inflation accounting, IAS 29 *Accounting in Hyperinflationary Economies*. The standard notes that it is a question of judgement as to what constitutes a hyperinflationary economy, but generally this is one where the value of the currency unit is diminishing sufficiently fast as to make year on year comparisons meaningless. It adds by way of a practical guideline (drawn from US GAAP) that inflation of 100% over three years would normally be regarded as sufficient to require use of this standard.

The standard notes that it is a question of judgement as to what constitutes a hyperinflationary economy

In headline terms, the standard requires financial statements to be prepared using the measurements at the end of the reporting period. The comparative figures have also to be re-stated to the currency value at the end of the reporting period. Monetary amounts are not re-stated unless there are contractual requirements for the amounts to move in response to inflation. Non-monetary amounts have to be re-stated using a general price index or using estimates where no index is available. The counterpart of the restatement is taken to the income statement as a separate component of the profit and loss for the year.

Conclusion

This chapter has reviewed revenue recognition and some other standards that relate to the income statement (while also potentially relating to the balance sheet). Some of the standards mentioned in this chapter were written quite a number of years ago and the contrast with more recent ones is quite strong. The IASB is well on the way to developing a new revenue recognition standard that should be used also in the US. It is also working on its own industry-specific standards in the area of insurance and mineral extraction, although these are probably some years away from application.

CHAPTER 5

BALANCE SHEET ITEMS

This chapter deals with standards that address major items in the Statement of Financial Position. It starts with property, plant and equipment, then investment property and leased assets. It then moves to intangible assets and mineral rights. The chapter looks at the standard on impairment and that on assets held for sale. It follows that with the treatment of financial instruments, disclosures of risks related to financial instruments, defining equity, liabilities and contingent liabilities.

In this chapter we will look at the standards governing the accounting treatment of the main balance sheet (Statement of Financial Position) line items for non-current assets, such as tangible assets, intangibles, and financial instruments, and also liabilities, as well as some current items. As noted in the previous chapter, labelling them as balance sheet items does not mean they do not have any impact on the income statement. Equally we will continue to refer to the financial statement as the balance sheet, although the US term statement of financial position is just as appropriate.

Property, plant and equipment

IAS 16 *Property, Plant and Equipment* is the basic standard that addresses this traditional area of the balance sheet – tangible assets. The standard builds in the conceptual framework definition by specifying that (IAS 16.7):

> *The cost of an item of property, plant and equipment shall be recognized as an asset if, and only if:*
> *(a) it is probable that future economic benefits associated with the item will flow to the entity; and*
> *(b) the cost of the item can be measured reliably.*

The standard (IAS 16.16) says that at initial recognition the asset should be measured at cost. It specifies that this should include its purchase price and also (a) any non-refundable duties and taxes, (b) costs attributable to bringing the asset to the location and condition necessary for it to operate (including site preparation, professional fees, etc.), and (c) the costs of subsequently dismantling the asset and restoring the site where the entity has an obligation to do that (dealt with in IAS 37, see below). It also specifies (IAS 16.19) that costs such as those of opening a new facility, or conducting business in a new location, or administration and general overheads are not to be capitalized into the asset.

The standard also addresses depreciation. A particularity of this is that it mandates the use of component depreciation. This is a requirement to look at an asset and consider whether there are any material components that have a useful life significantly different from that of the main asset. Typical examples would be an apartment block, where items such as lifts and communal heating equipment are likely to have a shorter life than the building itself. In such a case while the building might be depreciated at (say) 50 years, the lifts might be depreciated over 20 years and the heating over 10 years.

Depreciation is calculated after deducting an estimated residual value from the cost of the asset. The depreciable amount should then be allocated to 'reflect the pattern in which the asset's future economic benefits are expected to be consumed by the entity' (IAS 16.60). Depreciation should be re-assessed at least once a year and should consider expected usage, expected physical wear and tear, technical or commercial obsolescence and any legal limits. A change in the expected useful life of an asset is considered to be a 'change of estimates' rather than a change in accounting policy and as such does not call for a note disclosure.

Potential impairment is addressed in IAS 36, which we deal with below. It is worth mentioning also that the standard notes (IAS16.53) that the residual value deducted to reach the depreciable amount 'is often insignificant and therefore immaterial'. This is a broad hint to ignore residual values, and this is what many companies do in practice. It is fairly unusual to see a specific mention of materiality in a standard. The principle of materiality applies to all standards and so the IASB is normally reluctant to draw attention to it in particular cases.

> *Depreciation is calculated after deducting an estimated residual value from the cost of the asset*

Another particularity of IAS 16, and one which sometimes causes confusion, is that it allows subsequent measurement of tangible assets at valuation. The standard permits both a cost model and a revaluation model. IAS 16.31 specifies that where the revaluation model is chosen, any item of property, plant and equipment whose fair value can be measured reliably, should be valued at fair value, less any subsequent depreciation or impairment after the date of valuation. If you read IAS 16.31 in isolation, it appears to require the use of fair value, which may be one reason why some people have been known to describe the standard as a full fair value standard. However, IAS 16.29 makes it clear that there are two models, and the entity can choose **either** a cost approach **or** a revaluation approach.

IAS 16 was first issued in 1982 and pre-dated by more than a decade the growing interest in using fair value in the balance sheet as a systematic measurement basis. It did, however, follow closely a period of high inflation worldwide. In some countries that did not use any systematic approach to inflation accounting, revaluation of non-current assets was a relatively simple and effective way of compensating for the effects of inflation. In an economy where the unit of measure is losing its value, short-lived assets move up in price rapidly, but long-lived assets recorded at historical cost will progressively shrink in the balance sheet. Revaluing non-current assets helps combat this distortion of balance sheet ratios. In particular, revaluation of non-current assets was available in the UK and widely used at this time.

Inflationary conditions are probably the main reason for inclusion of this measurement base in IAS 16. The standard does not, differently from more recent fair value standards, require systematic remeasurement at each balance sheet date. It says fair value is normally determined through appraisal by professional valuers. The frequency of the valuation depends upon the changes in the fair values of the items being valued. Significant and volatile changes require annual revaluation but are not necessary otherwise. The standard suggests that revaluation on a three to five year cycle is acceptable where there are no volatile changes (IAS 16.34).

In the UK many companies revalued non-depreciable property only, and about every five years. It should be borne in mind that a professional appraisal would involve significant fees. Use of the revaluation model under IFRS is relatively rare.

For the sake of completeness, you should note that while IAS 16 is the base case for tangible non-current assets, there are special cases which have their own standards, including agricultural assets (see Chapter 4), leased assets, investment property, assets held for sale and mineral rights (dealt with below).

Investment property

The treatment of investment property is one of the obvious differences between IFRS and US GAAP. IAS 40 *Investment Property* allows companies a choice as to whether they account for an investment property at cost or at fair value. The fair value option allows companies to reflect gains and losses on the market value of their investments in the income statement, broadly in line with what is done for investments in equity.

The standard defines an investment property as:

> land or a building – or part of a building – or both, held (by the owner or by the lessee under a finance lease) to earn rentals or for capital appreciation or both, rather than for:
> (a) use in the production or supply of goods or services or for administrative purposes; or
> (b) sale in the ordinary course of business.

If a property is held partly as an investment property and partly for own use, the two parts are treated differently, provided that they could be sold separately. If they cannot be sold separately, then the property is accounted for under IAS 16, except where the own use part is insignificant.

At initial recognition, the property is measured at cost but thereafter the entity must opt for the historical cost model (IAS 16) or fair value. Property held under an operating lease but treated as an investment property must be measured at fair value. The same policy must be applied to all investment properties held by the entity. The standard also says that the fair value measurement must reflect market conditions at reporting date, which means that companies opting for the fair value model must value all of their properties every year. The fair value measurement does not take account of any costs to sell.

The standard also requires that a property is taken out of the investment property category if it ceases to be an investment property because it is to have construction work or to be sold or for any other reason. The IASB are aware that this requirement means that a company that decides to vacate an investment property held at fair value, refurbish it and then sell it, has to move from fair value (IAS 40) to cost (IAS 16) to fair value less costs to sell (IFRS 5) when it becomes available for sale (dealt with below).

the fair value measurement must reflect market conditions at reporting date

Leased assets

This is another contentious area of financial reporting. For many years, if you leased an asset, you recorded as an expense your regular rental payments and that was the end of the matter. However, in the 1980s it was recognized that from an economic perspective, leasing was just another form of asset financing. In many cases you gained control over an asset and you had a very real legal liability to pay rentals for however many years to come. The argument was that if you were representing the economic substance in preference to the legal form, you should show both a tangible asset and a lease liability in your balance sheet.

IAS 17 *Leases* is a standard that takes this view, and is similar in thrust to the US standard, SFAS 13. IAS 17 introduced the concept of the finance lease and the operating lease. An arrangement was a finance lease if the terms of the lease transferred 'substantially all the risks and rewards incidental to ownership'. In such a case you recognized the asset at inception of the lease, measured at the present value of the lease payments, using the discount rate inherent in the lease contract. You also recognize a lease liability for the same amount.

Subsequent to that, the asset is classified according to the nature of the physical asset and it is depreciated in the same way as other assets of the same class. The rental payment is split between interest on the outstanding liability and repayment of that liability.

IAS 17 and SFAS 13 set out to require lessees to show the leasing arrangement as a purchase with financing. However, this attempt to move finance on balance sheet has proved to be a failure. It defines what is a finance lease, and anything that fails that definition is an operating lease – still recording rental payments as an expense.

SFAS 13 set out clear criteria: the lease term had to be more than 75% of the expected life of the asset or the present value of the rental payments had to be more than 90% of the value of the asset. These clear targets made it relatively easy for the leasing industry to change the way they wrote their contracts. They used shorter lease terms and added in options to extend the lease, or issued a series of short leasing contracts, and failed the capitalization criteria.

IAS 17 is still in force, and while not many finance leases are to be found on balance sheets, some are seen. The standard does also include a disclosure of future lease rental commitments that give a user some idea of the extent of the leasing activity going on in the company.

However, the IASB and FASB are currently working on a radical new standard, for which an exposure draft was issued in 2010, although the final standard is not expected until late in 2011, probably for application in 2015. The new project abandons the notion of the split between operating leases and finance leases. It says **all** leases are by their nature a form of financing, and consequently an asset and a liability must be recognized.

However, there are a number of other changes as well. In particular the length of the leasing arrangement is not necessarily determined by the contract. The length has to be the period the entity **expects** to lease the asset, including renewals of the contract. Under the new arrangement another change is that the asset to be recognized will be an intangible – the right to use a physical asset, not the physical asset itself. Measurement will be at the present value of the contract, based on the lessee's marginal finance rate. However, contracts whose maximum length is not more than 12 months must still be recognized but need not be discounted.

In a slight reference to the old standard, where a lease gives the lessee the right to use the asset for virtually all its life, this is treated as a purchase and financing, and not a lease at all. The asset would be classified as a physical one.

Intangible assets

This area of IFRS accounting was substantially revised in 2003 to move IFRS into line with the changes in US GAAP on goodwill and business combinations. The basic approach of IAS 38 *Intangible Assets* is that only purchased intangibles are recognized, and their subsequent measurement may be on a cost basis or a valuation basis. In line with the Conceptual Framework, an intangible is recognized only if the entity has control over it, and if future economic benefits are expected to flow from it, and it can be measured reliably.

In addition to the standard asset definition, IAS 38 adds that an intangible must be separable or must arise from contractual or legal rights. Separability is the ability to sell or transfer the asset, either individually or in conjunction with another related asset or liability. If the asset is carried on a cost basis, it is subject to amortization and impairment. If it has a finite useful life, the cost is amortized over this and it is normally assumed that there is no residual value. If the asset is considered to have an indefinite useful life, then it is not amortized but it must be checked annually for impairment (as well as at any time there is an indication of impairment).

As regards specific kinds of asset, goodwill arising on consolidation is addressed in IFRS 3 *Business Combinations* and does not have to meet the IAS 38 criteria for an intangible asset (e.g. it is not separable, and some people do not think it is an asset, although the IASB's official position is that it **is** an asset). Goodwill must be tested for impairment annually and when there is any indication of impairment.

Research and development also falls under IAS 38. The requirements distinguish between the research phase and the development phase of a project. The research is expensed as incurred, but when the project has reached the point where there is a viable product that the entity has the resources to develop and believes can be commercially successful, it moves to development phase. The standard **requires** that development costs be capitalized.

In its original form, IAS 38 gave a choice of capitalizing or expensing development costs, but the IASB removed this when they revised the standard in 2003. This was thought by many to be an odd decision since the FASB requires that all research and development expenditure is taken immediately to the income statement. In addition, it creates the same tax issue as capitalizing interest – European companies would be more inclined to expense costs as incurred and take the tax deduction. Once they capitalize, the tax effect is deferred, consequently there is an incentive to use local GAAP for the statements of the subsidiary to get the tax benefit as early as possible.

Goodwill must be tested for impairment annually and when there is any indication of impairment

The application guidance for IFRS 3 makes it clear that a customer list acquired in a business combination would be considered to be a separable intangible, but the value of the assembled workforce (generally taken to be the cost of replacing the workforce) should not be recognized separately. However, internally generated intangibles are not recognized at the moment outside of a business combination. IAS 38 specifies: 'Internally generated brands, mastheads, publishing titles, customer lists and items similar in substance shall not be recognized as intangible assets'.

The IASB is aware that there is fundamental inconsistency in its approach to intangibles: purchased intangibles are recognized, while internally generated ones are not. By contrast, when accounting for tangible assets, both types are recognized. At one point they did have a project to develop a standard on recognition of internally generated intangibles. This was delegated to the Australian Accounting Standards

Board (AASB), but in the pressure of the financial crisis, the project was shelved for the time being and moved to the IASB's Research Agenda.

The AASB had prepared a discussion paper and this was published by the National Standard-Setters in 2008. Although the pressure on IASB time was a major consideration in putting the project aside, there was also feedback that some analysts did not think it was worth including the information. It was suggested that the analysts preferred to value unrecognized intangibles themselves and would disregard numbers produced by the reporting entity.

Mineral rights

One of the types of intangible excluded from IAS 38 is mineral rights. The issue here is that where a mining or exploration company conducts exploratory work towards identifying mineral resources, there is no specific expectation of future economic benefits arising from the work. There is a general expectation, but the purpose of the exploratory work is to establish whether or not there are benefits and in what quantity. The work done does not qualify as an asset in IAS 38 terms, and yet a mining company would probably be able to sell the information it has gained.

When the first wave of companies moved to IFRS in 2005, the IASB issued IFRS 6 *Exploration for and Evaluation of Mineral Resources*. The purpose of this standard was not to establish accounting rules for this, but rather to tell mining companies moving into IFRS that they should continue to use whatever accounting policy they had previously been using. Since then a number of National Standard-Setters (Australia, Norway, Canada and South Africa) have been working with the IASB to develop an IFRS that addresses this particular problem. They issued a discussion paper, *Extractive Industries*, which was published in 2010. The next stage will be a decision whether to take the project onto the IASB's active agenda. That should be taken in 2011, but it would likely be 2014 at the earliest before a final standard emerged.

Impairment

The rules for the impairment, or write-down, of non-current assets can vary significantly in national GAAP. Continental European countries with a Commercial Code typically have a requirement that, at each balance sheet date, the carrying value of an asset should not exceed its current value. However, some countries allow that an impairment is only recognized if it is thought that the loss of value is permanent, meaning that (say) a temporary drop in property prices would not necessarily trigger an impairment. Another issue that varies from asset to asset and country to country is the extent to which an impairment provision can be reversed subsequently.

The general standard in IFRS for impairment is IAS 36 *Impairment of Assets*. This applies to most non-current assets, but not to special assets such as financial instruments, investment property, inventory and agricultural assets. The basic rule is that the carrying value of an asset must not exceed its 'recoverable amount'. The recoverable amount is the higher of the fair value less costs to sell and cash flows realizable through use. In other words, as long as the entity thinks the asset could be turned into more cash than its accounting value, the accounting value is justified. If not, the accounting value must be reduced to the recoverable amount.

The standard does, however, introduce a concept that is not found in national law (although it is found in US GAAP). This is the Cash Generating Unit (CGU). The idea is that most assets other than financial instruments or investment property are not exploited alone, but are used as part of a group of assets that together form a business. Consequently, if one wants to measure their cash flows, one needs to take all the assets that are needed to generate cash flows. IAS 36 defines a CGU as 'smallest identifiable group of assets that generates cash inflows that are largely independent of the cash inflows from other assets or groups of assets'.

In practice it is not always that easy to identify what is a CGU. The standard gives examples such as a railway that is used uniquely to move ore from a mine to the commercial rail network, would have no individual fair value and no independent cash flows, but should be considered to be part of the mine CGU.

The impairment calculation in such a case is done in relation to the CGU, rather than in relation to the individual asset. The first step is for the entity to consider whether there is any indication that an asset is impaired. If there is none, unless another standard mandates it, there is no need to go into the impairment calculation. However, for assets such as goodwill and indefinite life intangibles, and assets where there is an indication, the impairment calculation involves estimating the amount that could be realized by selling the assets, less costs to sell, as well as the 'value in use'. The value in use is the present value of the cash flows that the CGU is expected to generate.

The standard specifies that the value in use includes the following elements:

(a) an estimate of the future cash flows the entity expects to derive from the asset;
(b) expectations about possible variations in the amount or timing of those future cash flows;
(c) the time value of money, represented by the current market risk-free rate of interest;
(d) the price for bearing the uncertainty inherent in the asset; and
(e) other factors, such as illiquidity, that market participants would reflect in pricing the future cash flows the entity expects to derive from the asset.

In practice there may not be that much difference between the fair value less costs to sell and the value in use. Fair value reflects the evaluation of the asset by market participants, and value in use is an evaluation based on management's expectations. Normally the management are expected to know more than the market (information asymmetry), but this does not necessarily mean they would value higher! Companies that prepare five or ten year budgets would probably use these to derive estimates.

For an asset that can be sold individually, a market price might be readily obtainable, but for a CGU, it is almost certain that there is no readily available market price, and fair value must be estimated using a present value model as in value in use. The only difference then would be that the fair value should reflect a market participant's views of likely cash flows. Nevertheless, in some areas of business there are valuation models widely used by selling agents, and these might be an appropriate way of finding a Level 3 fair value.

Fair value reflects the evaluation of the asset by market participants

Clearly when doing an impairment calculation, if the first alternative for recoverable amount turns out to be greater than the carrying value, there is no point in doing the second calculation.

However, if the recoverable amount turns out to be less than the carrying amount, an impairment provision must be passed to reduce the book value to the recoverable amount. The standard includes rules for how this is done. There is no difficulty if the impairment concerns a single asset, but where it relates to a CGU, there is an order in which the impairment is applied. Where the CGU has been acquired as part of a business combination, any goodwill recognized in the transaction has to be allocated to the CGUs (normally at the time of the acquisition). When an impairment is recognized, the provision is used first to write off the goodwill in the CGU. Once that has been done, any remaining provision is applied pro rata to the other assets.

By way of a simplified example, suppose that five years ago your company took over another company, one of whose CGUs was a motorway concession in Luxembourg. At the year end (20X0) the book values of the concession are as follows (€m):

Goodwill	15
Motorway	95
Less depreciation	−40
Current assets	10
Current liabilities	−5
Net assets	75

The motorway is being depreciated on the assumption of a 40-year life, with 23 years left to run. However, the Luxembourg government has announced a major restructuring of its motorway contracts, which is expected to start to take effect in five years. You expect that some compensation will be paid for cancelling the concession, but this is unlikely to be generous. A local company has offered to buy the concession for €50m. The management's estimates of the net present values of the cash flows from operations are:

20X1 €10m, 20X2 €8m, 20X 3 €6m, 20X4 €5m, 20X5 €25m

The total present value of these expected cash flows is €54m, and this compares with the market price of €50m (offer from local company). The recoverable amount is the higher of these: €54m. The carrying value of the CGU is €75m, so the impairment is €21m. This would be applied to the goodwill first and the remaining €6m would be deducted from the other non-current assets (€m):

Goodwill	0
Motorway	95
Less depreciation and impairment	−46
Current assets	10
Current liabilities	−5
Net assets	54

Once goodwill has been impaired, this can never be reversed. But other assets should be revisited. The entity is supposed to check whether its estimates of recoverable amount remain valid going forward. If the estimates change, because of changes in market conditions or other external factors, the recoverable amount should be recalculated and the impairment of any asset other than goodwill may be reversed.

Assets held for sale

The IASB withdrew their previous standard on this subject (IAS 35) in 2004 and replaced it with a standard (IFRS 5 *Non-current Assets held for Sale and Discontinued Operations*) that is intended to be closely aligned with those parts of the US SFAS 144 that address sales of parts of a business. The converged standard mandates that when a non-current asset or group of assets and liabilities ('a disposal group') is to be sold, the asset or disposal group will be classified separately in the balance sheet, valued at the lower of carrying value and fair value less costs to sell. The standard also requires that income from the asset or disposal group is shown separately in the income statement. The standard has the usual exceptions to its scope: it does not apply to financial instruments, insurance assets, deferred tax assets, agricultural assets, pension assets and investment properties accounted for at fair value.

A key issue is the point at which an asset shifts from being in current use to being accounted for as held for sale. The standard (IFRS5.6–8) says:

> An entity shall classify a non-current asset (or disposal group) as held for sale if its carrying amount will be recovered principally through a sale transaction rather than through continuing use.
>
> For this to be the case, the asset (or disposal group) must be available for immediate sale in its present condition subject only to terms that are usual and customary for sales of such assets (or disposal groups) and its sale must be highly probable.

> *For the sale to be highly probable, the appropriate level of management must be committed to a plan to sell the asset (or disposal group), and an active programme to locate a buyer and complete the plan must have been initiated. Further, the asset (or disposal group) must be actively marketed for sale at a price that is reasonable in relation to its current fair value.*

One particular detail caused some discussion when the IASB was debating this standard. IFRS 5 specifies that an asset or disposal group classified this way should no longer be depreciated. Some Board members thought that this opened the door to manipulation: if you had a bad year, you classified a poorly performing business as held for sale. That way you were able to strip out its result from the rest of operations and write back the year's depreciation. You could then continue to treat it as held for sale and not depreciate. In the end the IASB imposed a time limit – assets can only be classified this way for one year. If not sold by then, they are thrown back into the pool. When assets are withdrawn from sale, they are accounted for at the lower of their historical cost or their recoverable amount at the time of reclassification. The historical cost would be their carrying value before being classified as held for sale, adjusted for subsequent depreciation, etc.

Financial instruments

This highly controversial area is mostly irrelevant for the majority of commercial and industrial groups, while it is primordial for banks, insurance companies and other financial institutions. For the non-financial sector, the issue is that if they enter into any derivatives contracts (e.g. forward contracts on currencies or commodities), or they want to apply hedge accounting, or both, this standard concerns them. Receivables and payables generated by companies are not affected. However, it is also an area that is changing rapidly, as a result of pressures brought about by the financial crisis. Just to make life more complicated, it is an area where, famously, the IFRS as endorsed for use in the European Union do not correspond in all details with IFRS as issued by the IASB[1].

The need for a standard on financial instruments became apparent in the late 1980s when companies started to make a more widespread use of derivative contracts. Some of these turned into major losses that occurred without shareholders having any idea that the company was exposed to risk. The point with such contracts is that their historical cost is either nil or negligible and gives no inkling of the scale of risk. The solution found was to value them at market value at reporting date (in the same way as foreign currency balances). On the good side, this drew attention to their existence; on the bad side, companies complained that this was importing market volatility into their financial statements, and the real value would only be known when the contract was sold or matured.

The need for a standard on financial instruments became apparent in the late 1980s

The IASC started work on this in 1988, largely following in the footsteps of the FASB. It took the IASC practically until midnight on 31 December 1998 (see Chapter 9 for the significance of the deadline) to finalize a recognition and measurement standard, which became IAS 39. This was labelled an 'interim'

---

1 European banks have never liked IAS 39 and they lobbied the European Commission and the IASB for some changes. In particular they did not like the restriction (called the 'demand deposit floor') that said a liability cannot be measured at less than the amount that must be refunded on demand. Retail banks hold large amounts in customer current accounts which are in effect free financing for the bank. While these are churning all the time, in aggregate they are stable, and banks prefer to discount the liability. IAS 39 does not permit this, so when the Commission endorsed IAS 39 for use in the EU (EU law requires standard by standard endorsement) they removed the paragraph on this subject. This is known as the 'IAS 39 carve-out'. EU companies have to assert that they comply with IFRS 'as endorsed by the EU'. The SEC, however, does not recognize these, and only recognizes IFRS as issued by the IASB.

standard, and when the IASB took over in 2001, one Board member even suggested that the IASB should omit the standard from its blanket endorsement of the IASC's existing standards for that reason. Much of the standard remains in force still.

IAS 39 *Financial Instruments: Recognition and Measurement* is generally thought to be a very complicated standard. In an old hard copy of the standard on my bookshelves, the standard together with its Basis for Conclusions, implementation guidance, etc., runs to 368 pages. Sir David Tweedie (IASB chairman 2001–2011) was fond of joking: 'If anyone says they understand IAS 39, they haven't read it properly'. He also used to remark that IAS 39 should only be one page saying: all financial instruments should be at fair value. The rest of it is the exceptions that were negotiated. IAS 39 calls for financial assets to be classified in one of four categories: (1) loans and receivables not held for trading (accounted for at historical cost); (2) held to maturity investments (also accounted for at historical cost); (3) available for sale financial assets (measured at fair value, with changes in fair value flowing through Other Comprehensive Income); and (4) assets held for trading (measured at fair value with changes flowing through profit and loss). Financial instruments had to be classified at inception.

In 2008 the IASB's IAS 39, and the FASB's various financial instruments standards, started to be blamed, first by banks, and then by regulators and governments for being a cause of the financial crisis or at least exacerbating the crisis. People argued that on the upswing, banks had notched up huge unrealized profits on financial instruments valued at fair value, and expanded their lending. In the downswing they notched up huge fair value losses as the market went into freefall, and went bankrupt or had to be recapitalized. The standard-setters took the view that their standards were simply doing their job, giving up to date economic information which reflected, in this case, bankers' poor investment decisions.

Whatever the truth, the practical effect was that the G20 governments mandated the Financial Stability Board (group of banking regulators and others concerned with financial markets) to oversee, among other things, a review of the IASB and FASB standards, simplification and convergence. On top of this the IASB had to contend with the European Union telling it to make concessions, or the EU would unilaterally modify IFRS for European purposes.[2] The result of this pressure was that both the FASB and IASB made haste to amend their literature, although they unfortunately, as at the time of writing, did not reach the same conclusions, so divergence rather than convergence appears to be the likely outcome.

The IASB committed itself to fully replacing IAS 39, but doing this in stages. In 2009 it issued IFRS 9 *Financial Instruments*, which is to be the replacement standard. This first part addressed only financial assets and mandated that there should be two categories: debt instruments which were being held for their contractual cash flows, and all other instruments. Instruments in the first category are to be accounted for on a cost basis, while those in the second are accounted for at fair value through profit and loss.

A 2010 measure added liabilities to IFRS 9. This requires those accounted for at fair value to put fair value changes through profit and loss, but in a second stage, the change in fair value attributable to own credit risk would be backed out of income and be transferred to Other Comprehensive Income. Liabilities are only accounted for at fair value as an optional choice to be used when the liabilities are matching assets held at fair value.

Where a liability has an embedded derivative, the derivative should be separated from the liability ('bifurcated') and be accounted for at fair value. The IASB is projecting issue of a completed version of IFRS 9 by the end of 2011. This would preserve the derecognition requirements of IAS 39 but introduce new impairment and hedging requirements. The application date of the new standard has not been announced but would likely be 2015 or 2016.

---

2 For a detailed analysis of this, see André, P., Cazavan-Jeny, A., Dick, W., Richard, C. & Walton, P. (2009), 'Fair value accounting and the banking crisis in 2008: shooting the messenger', *Accounting in Europe*, 6: 3–24.

Hedging has historically been regarded with suspicion by some standard-setters

Hedging has historically been regarded with suspicion by some standard-setters on the basis that (a) they think that the hedged item and the hedging instrument should be accounted for separately (e.g. the accounting for an asset should not be different depending on whether it has been hedged or not), and (b) hedge accounting has been used selectively in the past to allow companies to recognize gains at once and defer losses. Consequently there are many hurdles to jump through in order to obtain hedge accounting, and the accounting itself is complicated.

IAS 39 allows a company to do hedge accounting for fair value hedges and cash flow hedges, but does not accept hedges for risk or for internal transactions (problematic for companies that operate internal netting of foreign exchange risk through central treasury). The hedged item and the hedging instrument have to be designated at inception and the designation has to be documented. Where the hedging instrument is a derivative or otherwise at fair value, the fair value changes for a cash flow hedge are taken to Other Comprehensive Income, and are then 'recycled' back to profit and loss when the hedged item matures. For a fair value hedge, fair value changes in both the hedging instrument and the hedged item are taken to profit and loss.

Hedges are required to be 'highly effective', otherwise their designation is cancelled and changes go to profit and loss independently. Highly effective means that the hedging instrument moves within a band of 80–125% of the hedged item (but note that the hedge could be of only a limited portion of the hedged item).

An exposure draft on hedge accounting was issued at the end of 2010, to become ultimately part of the IFRS 9 standard. This is expected to try to simplify hedge accounting by moving to a single model from the two in IAS 39, and by abandoning the effectiveness requirements. The

Board are told that the effectiveness requirements make it very difficult for companies to use hedge accounting for commodities. An example often cited is that you cannot buy futures on aviation fuel but airlines buy oil futures as an indirect hedge. However, as they are not totally correlated, they can become ineffective in IAS 39 terms.

Disclosures about financial instruments

It is worth mentioning that the IASB has a separate standard on disclosures related to financial instruments. IFRS 7 was issued in 2005 to replace IAS 30 that addressed the financial statements of banks, and the disclosure requirements of IAS 32 which was the first standard to address financial instruments (see below). The standard requires an entity to discuss its exposure to risks arising from financial instruments. It applies to all entities that apply IFRS and all financial instruments, so a manufacturer with no derivatives contracts would still need to discuss the risks associated with receivables and payables. However, the standard is mostly aimed at financial institutions and ensuring that they provide adequate disclosures of risk. According to feedback reported by staff during the financial crisis, the standard was perceived by users to have stood up to the test of that crisis and only a little tweaking was done.

The IASB sums up the standard as follows (IFRS 7.IN5):

> The IFRS requires disclosure of:
>   (a) The significance of financial instruments for an entity's financial position and performance.
>   (b) Qualitative and quantitative information about exposure to risks arising from financial instruments, including specified minimum disclosures about credit risk, liquidity risk and market risk. The qualitative disclosures describe management's objectives, policies and processes for managing those risks. The quantitative disclosures provide information about the extent to which the entity is exposed to risk, based on information provided internally to the

entity's key management personnel. Together, these disclosures provide an overview of the entity's use of financial instruments and the exposures to risks they create.

The exceptions in the standard relate to pensions, share-based payments, insurance contracts and investments in other companies that are included in the consolidation. The standard includes a long list of disclosures by class of financial instrument. This includes details of any defaults, pledges for collateral, reclassification between categories, etc.

Defining equity

IAS 32 *Financial Instruments: Presentation* is a standard that has had a somewhat contested history, but apparently remains difficult to replace. To paraphrase Winston Churchill, one might say it is the worst way of distinguishing debt from equity, apart from all the other ways. The standard was first issued in 1995 as the first part of the IASC's financial instruments project (discussed above). As originally issued it dealt with the debt/equity divide, and minimum disclosures about financial instruments. The disclosures have been moved into IFRS 7 and IAS 32 has otherwise been revisited a number of times, most recently in 2008.

The fundamental dividing line that the standard establishes is that something can only be classified as equity if there is no contractual requirement to deliver cash or another asset to the holder – everything else is a liability, and the balance sheet must distinguish clearly between the two categories. It may be worth pointing out that the IASB also specifies that minority interests (or 'non-controlling interests' in IFRS terms) should be shown as a separate category of shareholders' equity, and not be shown, as many companies used to do, as a third financing category.

When the standard started to be applied much more widely, in 2005, the IASB was made aware of a thorny problem that started out as the New Zealand farm cooperative problem and later extended to be also the German limited partnership problem. The New Zealand standard-setter pointed out that in its jurisdictions it had agricultural cooperatives where farmers had to become members to do business with the cooperative, and had to sell back their shares to the cooperative when they no longer wanted to do business. The cooperative would buy the shares back at proportionate fair value.

If you apply IAS 32 as written to these cooperatives, all of the equity becomes a liability, because the entity can be required contractually to make a payment. Initially this means that the cooperative has no equity, and then if it makes a profit, this makes the cooperative apparently insolvent. As profit is made, this increases the liability to members because their payment is calculated at fair value. However, the cooperative is reporting on a historical cost basis so the increase in the value of the liability shows up as a loss.

When the IASB started to debate this issue, it then emerged that German limited partnerships could have the same problem. In such arrangements the limited partners are not allowed to sell their share of the partnership to an outsider; they are obliged to put them back to the partnership. While the buy back number is not necessarily at fair value, it was argued that the buy back reflected the growth in the wealth of the partnership during the period that the retiring member had held a share.

The IASB scratched its collective head and decided that, given that there was a joint project with the FASB to revisit the debt/equity issue, the best solution was to issue an amendment creating an exception to the basic rule, and deal with the problem on a more permanent basis in the joint project.

The result was the 2008 amendment, which allowed such arrangements to be treated as equity, subject to attempted ring-fencing which specified that the class of equity had to be the residual risk-taker, and that all shares in that class had the same proportionate interest. Those among the IASB who worried most about potential abuse saw the exception otherwise as creating an opening for super-shares that could be put back to the company at any time, and creaming off profits before they reached the general shareholders.

The joint project in which the IASB put their faith for the long term is labelled *Financial Instruments with the Characteristics of Equity* (FICE), which was included in the Memorandum of Understanding (MoU) target for completion by June 2011. In June 2010 the two standard-setters said they were deferring this target until the end of 2011, officially to reduce the burden on constituents of addressing a large amount of new material at the same time.

Observers are sceptical that this project will achieve anything. The FASB had been working on it for years before it became a joint project, and was stuck with the problem that if you try to make it a standard with a fundamental principle, the definition of equity is either too narrow or too wide to suit constituents. If you try to hit in between, you end up with a rule-based standard, going through the range of financial instruments and picking which falls on which side of the line – and leaving room for somebody to find new ones that cross the line.

The staff have brought many, many papers to the Boards and no approach commands a majority with both Boards. Not least, the IASB cannot accept a standard that does not address the New Zealand/ German problem, but no one can find a principle that covers that approach and does not create all sorts of 'structuring opportunities'. In theory IAS 32 will be replaced in the medium term, but we would not like to forecast when, nor, if it is replaced, that the new standard will look much different.

At a detailed level, IAS 32 requires that a financial instrument is classified as debt or equity at inception and not subsequently reclassified. Where an instrument contains an embedded derivative (e.g. convertible debt) the derivative has to be separated out (bifurcated) and is accounted for at fair value. The host contract is measured at cost less the initial fair value of the derivative. Treasury shares (shares in itself bought by the company) are accounted for solely within equity. Any profits or losses made from dealing in treasury shares remain in equity and do not flow through the income statement. Costs of issuing shares – other than in a business combination – are deducted directly from equity.

Liabilities

Plain vanilla liabilities are usually accounted for at amortized cost, but IAS 39 provides an option to measure at fair value under restricted conditions where they are matching assets valued at fair value (see section on financial instruments above). The standard that addresses non-financial liabilities is IAS 37, currently labelled *Provisions, Contingent Liabilities and Contingent Assets* and currently the subject of proposed amendments.

Leaving aside contingent items for the time being, the basic principle of the standard is (IAS 37.14):

> *A provision shall be recognized when:*
> *(a) an entity has a present obligation (legal or constructive) as a result of a past event;*
> *(b) it is probable that an outflow of resources embodying economic benefits will be required to settle the obligation; and*
> *(c) a reliable estimate can be made of the amount of the obligation.*
> *If these conditions are not met, no provision shall be recognized.*

Applying the standard calls for a high degree of judgement. The first issue is whether an obligation exists. The requirement for there to be an obligation can be seen as an anti-abuse measure that is designed to limit the practice of creating unnecessary provisions in good times to release them later (known as 'cookie jar provisions' in the US literature) as part of an earnings management process.

Applying the standard calls for a high degree of judgement

The standard itself (IAS 37.70–83) goes into detail about the point at which an entity may conclude it has a constructive obligation to provide for future restructuring charges. This can only be done when the entity has worked out a detailed plan, the board has agreed it and the main points have been communicated to those concerned. In other words, the entity cannot decide in December 2009 that it will restructure in 2010 and create a provision in the 2009 statements to provide a cushion for 2010.

Nonetheless the nature of the 'constructive obligation' can cause debate. The payment of a dividend is not considered to be a constructive obligation, even if the entity has paid a dividend for the last 50 years. In debates about their insurance contracts project, the question arises in a participating life insurance contract where the policyholder shares in the investment returns on the portfolio (sometimes known as a 'with profits' policy). The IASB ruled that if the policy gave the policyholder a legal entitlement to a specified share of profits, that obligation could be recognized. However, if the amount of profits shared with policyholders was at the insurer's discretion, no provision could be made, even if the insurer could point to the fact that they regularly paid out a certain amount.

In debating amendments to IAS 37, the IASB endlessly discussed the case of the hamburger restaurant. If, statistically, one in every 100,000 hamburgers is contaminated, the eater suffers food-poisoning, and the seller pays €20,000 compensation, should you make a provision when you have sold 100,000 hamburgers? The IASB decided in the end that you did **not** make a provision, because this was a business risk, and you had no knowledge that you had actually sold a contaminated burger. IAS 37 requires an event to have taken place, not the likelihood of an event.

This contrasts with guarantees and warranties, where they argue that suppliers mostly have either contractual or statutory obligations to replace or repair faulty goods or compensate for faulty services. In this case there is a legal obligation and you are entitled to create a provision based on a statistical probability derived from past experience.

Another difficult area is that of litigation. The IASB asked lawyers to talk to it about the impact of IAS 37 in this area. They said that in most cases it was quite impossible to estimate the liability, and even if you could, it was potentially prejudicial to the client to make any comment. A provision to settle a legal claim would undoubtedly be cited by the plaintiff as an admission of liability. Companies mostly resolve the problem of compliance with IAS 37 by claiming that they cannot make a reliable estimate.

The standard specifies that you cannot anticipate future losses by provisioning but you are required to provide for future costs in relation to **onerous contracts**. IAS 37.68 says:

> *This Standard defines an onerous contract as a contract in which the unavoidable costs of meeting the obligations under the contract exceed the economic benefits expected to be received under it. The unavoidable costs under a contract reflect the least net cost of exiting from the contract, which is the lower of the cost of fulfilling it and any compensation or penalties arising from failure to fulfil it.*

The next controversial part of the standard is the measurement of the liability. The principle is (IAS 37.36): 'The amount recognized as a provision shall be the best estimate of the expenditure required to settle the present obligation at the end of the reporting period'. The standard goes on to add (IAS 37.37): 'The best estimate of the expenditure required to settle the present obligation is the amount that an entity would rationally pay to settle the obligation at the end of the reporting period or to **transfer it to a third party** at that time' (emphasis added).

Some of the members of the IASB (notably Sir David Tweedie) were part of the group that drew up IAS 37 in the 1990s, and they agree that what they meant was that the provision should be measured at fair value, but they did not want to express it that way. However, as practice has developed, companies are believed to give their best estimate as to what they expect to pay when the liability falls due, and then discount back.

Currently the IASB take the view that this approach is wrong, the standard is specific that the measurement is what it would cost to settle **today** or what you would pay to transfer to someone else today. They have published an amendment which makes this clear and specifies that it is the transfer notion that is paramount. This should be computed by taking a probability weighted estimate of likely outcomes, discounting for uncertainty and making allowance for a risk margin, which would be required by a third party to take on the risk.

Respondents to the exposure draft such as the European Financial Reporting Advisory Group (the European Commission's technical advisor on IFRS) have commented that (a) these liabilities are nearly always settled and not transferred, (b) the best estimate of the future settlement approach has not caused any problems in practice, (c) they do not see that this change will improve financial reporting. It remains to be seen whether the IASB sticks to its proposed amendment or not. It decided in 2010 to put the work to one side because of the need to focus on convergence topics for issue in 2011. They will start work on the amendments again after 2011.

Contingent liabilities

The same standard is involved in a second and unrelated controversy about contingent liabilities and assets. The standard says that a contingent liability is a possible liability that does not meet the recognition criteria for a provision. A contingent liability is an obligation whose existence is not yet certain and is subject to some further event taking place, or it is less than probable that it will crystallize, or the amount is too uncertain to be recognized. A contingent liability under IAS 37 gives rise to a disclosure in the notes to the financial statements indicating its existence. At the moment many companies that operate in the US deal with ongoing litigation in this way.

However, the IASB's proposed amendments to IAS 37 include a proposal to abandon contingent liabilities and assets as a separate item. The staff argument is that a contingent liability can be broken down into two elements: (1) an actual liability, and (2) a probability of it maturing, which should be recognized and measured at its expected value. For example, a legal claim for €100,000 following an industrial accident, which has a 20% chance of being awarded by the courts, should under the proposal be seen as requiring a provision of €20,000, rather than being an unrecognized contingent liability disclosure.

This proposal has not been enthusiastically received by commentators either. As is fairly usual with expected values, people say they are meaningless since they do not represent a possible outcome. In the example above, people would say the outcome is either €100,000 or zero. The response is that in a large company the aggregate expected outcomes of the many uncertainties should approximate to the actual outcomes in total. As discussed above, the IASB has put the project to one side for the moment, although it seems likely that the more likely than not threshold will be preserved.

Conclusion

This chapter has made a brief tour of the main standards impacting balance sheet presentation. It has tried to focus on aspects of IFRS that are not routinely found in national GAAP or that are currently subject to change. In particular the area of accounting for financial instruments is undergoing radical review and is likely to continue to change. The nature of change is also less predictable in this area because of the potential involvement of political pressures, and of the problem of convergence between two groups with fairly different views.

the area of accounting for financial instruments is undergoing radical review

CHAPTER 6

OTHER SIGNIFICANT STANDARDS

This chapter brings in a series of other standards whose subject matter did not seem to fit naturally into the income statement or statement of financial position approach. The subjects dealt with are first time adoption, related party transactions, segment reporting, concessions, events after the reporting date and insurance.

This chapter looks at a number of standards that potentially need to be considered by any company using IFRS, but that do not fit obviously into the balance sheet or income statement chapters above. The subjects that you will find in this chapter are first time adoption, related party transactions, segment reporting and concessions.

First time adoption

This is a very significant standard, but one that most companies only get to apply once (although the IFRS Interpretations Committee in 2010 came to the conclusion that it was possible to have to apply it more than once if for some reason you left IFRS and then came back later). This standard, the first issued by the current standard-setter, sets out the basis on which people who are switching to IFRS from another GAAP should make the appropriate adjustments. IFRS 1 is a key standard in that companies very rarely get the opportunity to revisit all of their accounting policies, and careful thought is necessary so as not to waste that opportunity. First time adoption is a move to a new comprehensive basis of accounting. Often the new basis will not allow choices, but where it does, these need careful evaluation of their impact.

In headline terms, the standard says that you should adjust your existing figures to what they would have been had you always applied IFRS. However, it recognizes that in many cases this is impossible because you just would not have the data, or it is impractical because the costs of reconstituting the data outweigh the benefits. The IASB also systematically prohibits the use of hindsight in making restatements. Consequently the standard provides a useful collection of exceptions and workarounds which constitute this special opportunity, although changing estimates from those used in 'previous GAAP' is not encouraged. All of the changes are netted into a one time adjustment to retained earnings.

First time adoption is a move to a new comprehensive basis of accounting

You should also be aware that the standard in effect requires you always to convert your accounting in the year **before** the official change. IAS 1 requires that you provide one year's comparative figures, and so if the official conversion date is 2012, you actually have to be able to supply 2011 comparatives under IFRS. Consequently you have to run parallel systems for 2011. IFRS 1 would tell you to publish 2011 statements using previous GAAP, and then prepare 2011 statements using IFRS, as well as a reconciliation statement that gets you from one to the other. The reconciliation statement has to be published, and no later than the first statement that you publish under IFRS. So if you were converting officially in 2012, and published interim accounts, the reconciliation statement must appear by then. In practice many people publish the reconciliation ahead of that.

IFRS 1 *First Time Adoption of IFRS* was issued in 2003 and replaced a previous Interpretation. It has changed over time and was reformatted in 2008. It has been improved in the light of experience, and as new issues come to light. For example, Canada asked for an easing of requirements for valuing oil assets ahead of its 2011 adoption.

The basic requirements of the standard are (IFRS 1.10) that an entity shall in its opening statement of financial position:

(a) recognize all assets and liabilities whose recognition is required by IFRSs;

(b) not recognize items as assets or liabilities if IFRSs do not permit such recognition;

(c) reclassify items that it recognized in accordance with previous GAAP as one type of asset, liability or component of equity, but are a different type of asset, liability or component of equity in accordance with IFRSs; and

(d) apply IFRSs in measuring all recognized assets and liabilities.

The opening balance sheet is that of the first period where IFRS are applied. So in the example above of a 2012 public transition, the transitional balance sheet would actually be 1 January 2011, and this balance sheet would be reconciled to the previous GAAP figures. You should be aware that the transitional provisions of IFRS 1 override those of individual IFRS.

Appendices B, C and D of the standard address the various exceptions and concessions that are designed to make the transition easier to handle. Appendix C deals with business combinations. Generally the requirement is that a company may go back and restate business combinations to the extent it has the figures available, but must restate all business combinations forward from the date chosen. It may choose not to restate past business combinations. The goodwill figure retained for IFRS is then that of previous GAAP, except if previous GAAP recognized assets that are not recognized under IFRS. These are adjusted back into goodwill, and then goodwill is tested for impairment under IAS 36.

Appendix D is a collection of exemptions. These include the notion of 'deemed cost': the entity can decide to value property, plant and equipment, investment property and some intangible assets at fair value on transition, instead of trying to restate the numbers from previous GAAP. Where the entity has a defined benefit pension scheme, the accumulated actuarial differences should be taken to the transitional adjustment.

The question of not applying hindsight is covered in Appendix B. This says that the entity should **not** make retrospective adjustments to hedge accounting, financial assets and liabilities, derecognition and non-controlling interests.

Related party transactions

IAS 24 *Related Party Disclosures* is a standard that has had its troubles over the years. Its main thrust is that companies should disclose transactions with 'related parties', which could be human relationships with close family but also relationships with other companies that are owned by a common shareholder, etc. It does also mandate disclosure of the remuneration of key management personnel, and requires disclosure of parent/subsidiary relationships, even if there are no transactions.

The standard was first issued in 1984, but was slightly revised by the IASB in 2003. The revision, however, inadvertently created a significant issue for China, giving rise to a long series of papers and exposure drafts trying to address 'the Chinese problem'. This resulted in a new version in 2009.

In its earlier days, the main problem for IAS 24 was its requirement to disclose the remuneration of key management personnel. In some jurisdictions there is no legal requirement to disclose this information, or disclosures are limited to main board directors. Consequently when the EU decided to adopt IFRS from 2005, this meant, by way of example, that senior divisional managers, who had extremely advantageous packages that had never been revealed to shareholders, were reluctant to see this information published.

China has not directly adopted IFRS, but has been progressively aligning its domestic rules for listed companies on IFRS (this is also referred to by some as convergence, which can be confusing). Although it does not directly adopt IFRS, China takes careful note of the evolution of IFRS. Chinese officials pointed out that, if they applied the 2003 version of IAS 24 to their companies, every company would have to report nearly all its transactions as being with related parties. The issue is that nearly all major companies in China have some form of government stake, so, within the terms of the standard they are related parties. They also noted that in fact a company would not necessarily know that it was dealing with a related party.

They asked whether a company owned by a provincial government would be considered as a related party of a company owned by the national government, or indeed another provincial government. (IASB member Jim Leisenring summed this up as: 'If I buy electricity from the Michigan state power corporation, does this mean the US government is a related party?').

The IASB accepted that something had to be done, but crafting wording that avoided meaningless and unnecessary disclosures while not giving a blanket exemption for state-owned entities took several attempts and much head-scratching. As now written, the standard provides an exemption (IAS 24.25) for transactions with a government that has control, joint control or significant influence, and with other entities over which the same government has control, joint control and significant influence.

Where an entity claims the government exemption, it must then make a disclosure about the name of the government and the nature of the control, and the nature of any significant transactions. It provides guidance as to what might be significant transactions, including those carried out on non-market terms or outside the normal course of business, as well as just because of size considerations.

Segment reporting

IFRS 8 *Operating Segments* is the standard now in force that specifies the reporting of segment information by groups. The standard is a convergence one and its wording is exactly that of the US standard SFAS 131, apart from editorial changes to conform the vocabulary to IFRS terms instead of US GAAP ones. The standard applies only to listed groups and specifies what constitutes a reportable segment and what information should be provided. The key issues are that the information should be the same as that provided to the 'chief operating decision-maker' in a group. Consequently it may not be based on IFRS measurements, although it must be reconciled to the numbers in the financial statements.

The approach is known as 'through the eyes of management' and can be seen as an attempt to address information asymmetry by providing to investors the same information that management are using. It has a practical advantage that, as compared with the previous standard, it does not require the group to prepare special numbers that are used only for public reporting.

When IFRS 8 was introduced there was some pushback from European constituents. They pointed out that the previous standard (IAS 14) had mandated disclosures on both a geographical and a sectoral basis, and that the segments had to be calculated on the same basis as the published financial statement to which they referred. This meant, it was claimed, that there was much more comparability from one company to another – e.g. the car manufacturing activity of Daimler could be compared with the car manufacturing of Renault, without 'noise' from trucks, aircraft manufacture, etc.

Others took the view that, since the segment data under IAS 14 had no other purpose or use within the group, they were artificial – they were not necessarily decision-useful, could be drawn up under a number of different assumptions about how costs and revenues were allocated, and were costly to prepare. At least under IFRS 8 there was no pretence of comparability. The European parliament considered trying to block the standard in Europe, but eventually backed down under Commission pressure.

IFRS 8 came into force in January 2009. It defines an operating segment in terms of having its own revenues and expenses and being reported discretely to the chief operating decision-maker. The standard suggests that a segment typically has a segment manager who reports to the chief operating decision-maker. This approach is modified with the comment that activities that are aggregated into a reportable segment would be expected to have similar economic characteristics. There is also a quantitative threshold – anything that has more than 10% of sales, or 10% of profits or 10% of group assets will qualify as a segment.

When IFRS 8 was introduced there was some pushback from European constituents

The standard includes a list of quantitative disclosures including segment profit or loss, revenues from external customers, revenues from transactions with other segments, depreciation, interest, material items of income and expense relating to disposals and restructurings. If total assets and liabilities are reported to the chief operating decision-maker, these must also be provided to investors. Additions to non-current assets (excluding financial instruments and pensions) must also be reported.

The notes to the disclosure should explain the accounting policies that have been used in each of the segments, and the group must provide a reconciliation from the totals for revenue, net earnings and total assets in the segment disclosures to the totals in the group financial statements. IFRS 8 also mandates a minimum of information on revenues and non-current assets analysed by geographical area.

Concessions

One of the issues that faced the IASB when it came into being in 2001 was that it needed to make sure that its standards were suitable for European adoption in 2004/5. A gap that was identified was the lack of a standard for service concessions, or 'public to private' concessions. This is the provision, usually of some form of infrastructure, to a public authority by a private sector entity, in return for operating income. The infrastructure typically reverts to the public authority at the end of the contract. A typical example could be a motorway or a hospital. The advantage to the public body is that it gains the infrastructure without having to borrow money to finance its construction – it pays for it as it uses it. The Channel Tunnel was launched as exactly such a project where the private sector built and operates the tunnel, but ultimately ownership will revert to the British and French governments.

The IASB decided that it was not necessary to issue a standard to cover this: the topic could be dealt with as an Interpretation of existing standards. That choice was contested by some commentators, particularly the European Financial Reporting Advisory Group, who thought that the Interpretations Committee was in effect writing a new standard. Whatever one thinks about that, the rules are today to be found in Interpretation 12 *Service Concession Arrangements*.

The Interpretation uses the terms 'grantor' for the public authority issuing the concession, and 'operator' for the private entity that constructs and then operates the infrastructure. During the construction phase, the operator accumulates costs as a tangible non-current asset. When the infrastructure is ready to enter service, that asset disappears, to be replaced by either a financial asset or an intangible asset depending on the arrangement with the grantor. The Interpretation says that the operator is a service provider and is going to be paid either (a) directly by the public authority (in which case a financial asset representing the right to receive payment is recognized) or (b) by being allowed to charge users directly (in which case the operator has an intangible asset, the right to charge tolls).

The Interpretation was not well received in some quarters. Spanish infrastructure companies were in particular mobilized against it. The problem they saw was that if they built a motorway and then operated it through charging tolls for a period of time, they would end up with an intangible asset, where previously they would have recognized the motorway as a tangible non-current asset. They usually borrowed the money to finance such arrangements, and their lenders would see the intangible as more risky than the tangible. In addition, the interest charged would be accumulated as part of the intangible asset and run off over the service period, rather than being expensed in the construction phase.

Events after balance sheet date

There is a standard, IAS 10 *Events after the Reporting Period*, which addresses the action to be taken if a significant event occurs between the balance sheet date and the day the directors sign off the annual accounts. Many large multinationals try to publish their accounts in under three months from the balance sheet date, so the window of time for these events is only a few weeks. In essence the standard says that if an event occurs that sheds light on the situation at the year end, the figures must be adjusted. If the event will impact the following year and is material, it should be disclosed. The footnotes should specify at what date the accounts were authorized for issue, so that users can know what was the period during which such events should have been reported. The standard specifies that a decision to pay a dividend taken after balance sheet date does not result in recognition of a liability. However, a perception that the company is no longer a going concern could be a reason to go back and remeasure at balance sheet date.

IAS 10 had its name changed when the IASB decided to start calling the balance sheet the statement of financial position. Its terms distinguish between 'adjusting events' and 'non-adjusting events'. An adjusting event is one that gives additional information about the situation at the previous year-end. For example, the settlement of a legal claim that was represented by a provision in the balance sheet would cause the company to true-up the provision to the settlement amount.

A non-adjusting event is one that gives information about the subsequent evolution of the company's affairs since balance sheet date. Such an event could be the acquisition of another company. If the event is material in terms of understanding the company's future, it must be disclosed in the notes to the accounts, but does not have any impact on the published figures. The only exception to this is the case of ceasing to be a going concern. IAS 10.14 says that if, after the balance sheet date, the management decide to cease trading or that there is no realistic possibility of continuing, they should not issue the financial statements on a going concern basis.

Insurance

There is an insurance standard in force, IFRS 4 *Insurance Contracts*, but the main thrust of this is to allow companies to continue with their pre-IFRS GAAP. The standard deals with **contracts** as opposed to insurance companies on the basis that an insurance company might have several lines of business and that many of its assets and liabilities are covered by other standards, notably IFRS 9 on financial instruments. Equally it is hard to define what is meant by an insurance company.

The increasing globalization of business has led companies in different parts of the world but in the same business sector to converge their financial reporting to a degree so that their statements are comparable. The great exception to this is the insurance sector, where different countries have developed quite different approaches and retained them. This is, then, a sector where an international standard-setter could give a lead, and the old IASC started a project which it passed on to the IASB in 2001.

The IASB has devoted countless hours to this subject, but its initial work was greeted with a good deal of opposition by the different major players in the field. After a couple of years of getting nowhere, the IASB realized that it would not finish a standard in time for major European insurers to use in 2004/5. It decided therefore to issue an interim standard. Had it not done so, insurers would in theory have been obliged to follow the hierarchy for accounting policy choice from IAS 8.

In the absence of an IFRS, the hierarchy would take them to national standards which were set using the same conceptual framework. In this case that would take them to US GAAP or eventually Australian GAAP. In effect they would have to move from previous GAAP to (say) US GAAP and subsequently to IFRS when the standard was completed. Insurers would have had two forced changes of accounting so the IASB issued IFRS 4, which suspended the policy hierarchy for insurers and let them carry on using previous GAAP.

it is hard to define what is meant by an insurance company

The IASB did, however, impose some limitations by forbidding the use of 'catastrophe provisions'. Some insurers build provisions against major catastrophes where they don't routinely get claims every year. However, this offends the IASB principle that you do not anticipate future expenses: you tell the situation how it is today! IAS 37 specifies that a provision must arise as a result of some **past** event, and not a future event. The insurance contracts standard also requires companies to carry out a liability adequacy test, and not to offset insurance assets against insurance liabilities.

Having issued IFRS 4, the IASB then reverted to working on the substantive insurance standard. The world's major insurers started to become more engaged in the project, including the US companies such as AIG. The FASB did not participate in the project at this stage, but when the IASB issued a discussion paper in May 2007, the FASB also put out the paper in the US. Subsequently the FASB decided that it wanted this to be a joint project, and as a consequence progress, already faltering, has slowed.

A central problem for standard-setters is that they mostly would like insurance accounting to be much like any other accounting, and it takes a good deal of reflection and discussion to accept that that is very difficult. This is not least because insurance works in the opposite way to most business – first you get the money, and then you get the expenses. Even on a portfolio of one year policies, there may be some claims that arise several years afterwards, and few are settled in the year when cover is being provided.

The involvement of the FASB in the project has meant revisiting a number of decisions that had been painstakingly worked out in the past. Consequently the exposure draft only emerged in the second half of 2010. The IASB still targets issuing a final standard by June 2011 (when the present chairman stands down) but this looks optimistic, especially if it should be a joint standard. One could imagine the new standard being in force by about 2014 or 2015, having been well over a decade in the making.

Conclusion

This chapter has had a look at a series of disparate standards, all, except for insurance, are likely to affect multinational companies but not all smaller companies. A key standard is IFRS 1, which says how a company adjusts its previous accounting when it moves to using IFRS as its comprehensive basis of accounting. Most companies will, of course, only use this standard once, but the decisions to be taken are significant.

CHAPTER 7

THE IFRS FOR SMES

This chapter completes the review of IFRS as such and addresses the separate standard that is intended to meet the needs of small and medium-sized businesses. The chapter explains the origins of the project and analyses the content of the standard as well as drawing attention to the small number of areas where its requirements differ from those of IFRS for listed companies.

This ground-breaking standard was issued in 2009 and sits apart from the body of IFRS. It provides a stand-alone comprehensive basis of accounting for small and medium-sized businesses and has been adopted in many countries for companies in a size tier below that in which IFRS are used. Essentially the standard has been created from all the other IFRS. It has been made much shorter partly by eliminating rules for transactions it was thought an SME would be unlikely to have, partly by simplifying the language and partly by introducing some simplified accounting. It includes a version of the conceptual framework and runs to just under 230 pages. It can be used by private companies that are subsidiaries of listed companies, as well as independent private companies.

The standard is organized by topic and has some 35 chapters. It starts with concepts and principles, goes on to financial statement presentation and then looks at each of the financial statements, followed by a series of accounting issues. The standard is supported by a dedicated team at the IASB, headed by Dr Paul Pacter, who was in charge of the preparation of the standard, and is now a Board member. The staff at the IASB provide a monthly newsletter to which those who are interested in the standard have free access.

Because the standard is drawn from full IFRS, it will need to evolve over time as IFRS evolve. However, this is to be done on a systematic basis, once every two years, rather than on a piecemeal basis. Changes in IFRS will be reviewed and amendments proposed once every two years by the SMEs Implementation Group (SMEIG).

Development of the standard

The idea of doing a separate standard for SMEs was quite controversial for the IASB in as far as it was focused on reporting by listed companies. On top of that, once work started there was subsequently a great deal of debate about what should be the relationship with full IFRS and if any recognition and measurement concessions could be made.

The idea of doing such a project had been taken up by the IASC, which had even set up a working group. Consequently, back in 2001 in the early days of the IASB, the new organization considered whether to carry on with the project. At the time there was little enthusiasm, and the project did not get under way until 2003. There was a demand for accounting rules for SMEs coming from a number of sources. Developing countries wanted a ready-made set of accounting rules that were suitable for local business. IFRS as such were considered to be too sophisticated for most companies in such countries. At the same time the European Commission also thought that it would be useful to have rules for smaller companies that meshed with IFRS so that growing companies would have a logical progression.

In the late 1990s the UN's Intergovernmental Group of Accounting Experts on International Standards of Accounting and Reporting (ISAR) was receiving a lot of calls for guidelines to be provided to deal with accounting in developing countries. Although ISAR is committed to working with IFRS, at that time the IASC had no plan to work in this area. Consequently ISAR did some research that was published in 2000 on the accounting needs of smaller businesses in developing countries. This recommended a three-tier system, with IFRS for the largest companies, a cut-down form for smaller companies, and a simple form of accruals accounting for very small units. ISAR subsequently went ahead and developed its SMEGA (guidelines for SMEs, based on simplified IFRS) and its guidelines for the smallest units.

The standard is supported by a dedicated team at the IASB

The fact that institutions such as the United Nations were starting to address accounting for SMEs caused the IASB to review the urgency of the question. As Tom Jones, then deputy chairman of the IASB, remarked, 'if anyone is going to edit our standards, it had better be us'. Not everyone on the Board agreed. The constitution at the time specified that the IASB should write standards for the international capital markets. Tony Cope, an analyst member of the Board, considered that they therefore had no mandate to address SMEs.

Other members were concerned that in the late 1990s the IASC had had to fight against companies making a partial adoption of standards. They claimed to follow international accounting standards but then limited the ones they actually followed, often avoiding compliance with the pensions' standard and with remuneration disclosures under IAS 24. This came to be known as 'IAS Lite' and did some damage to the IASC. The successor Board did not want itself to be introducing something that could be labelled 'IFRS Lite'.

Another issue, not discussed by the Board, was whether they had any specialist knowledge useful in writing such a standard, given that they had all been appointed because of their knowledge of reporting in the international capital markets. In any event, Dr Pacter, who had served on the staff of the FASB and the IASC in the past, was drafted in from Hong Kong as Director of SME Accounting to lead the project.

One of the areas of disagreement among people who want accounting rules for SMEs is the nature of the SME and the economic environment within which it works. In particular there is a potential conflict between the needs of entities in a developed economy, supported by sophisticated accounting and finance infrastructure, as against those in a developing economy. The UN guideline had no mention of group accounts, defined benefit pensions plans or derivatives and other sophisticated financial instruments. The IFRS for SMEs includes all of these, suggesting that it was written more with a developed economy in mind.

Another key issue is whether the SME standard should be a stand-alone document or should include fallbacks to full IFRS (the 'Big Book' as Board members liked to refer to it). The IASB issued a Discussion paper in June 2004 that asked for feedback on these issues and on questions of whether the Board should issue such a standard, and whether it should permit derogations from the requirements of IFRS.

This led to confirmation that the project would go ahead. Dr Pacter then took the unusual step of sending out a questionnaire asking what issues needed simplification, what issues needed measurement advice for SMEs and what issues could be omitted. This was also used as the basis of round tables.

On the basis of this feedback the Board re-deliberated and the staff started to prepare an exposure draft. This was finally issued in February 2007. Some Board members were not happy with the content, and in the end Jim Leisenring, a former member of the FASB, who had opposed any recognition and measurement changes, dissented. Board members agreed that in drawing up the proposal, they were thinking in terms of an entity with 50 employees. They did not impose any size constraints, but the final standard is not meant for a micro-business. Once the exposure draft was published, it was subjected to significant field testing in a number of countries.

During 2008 the Board re-deliberated the issues in the light of the feedback from the exposure draft and the field tests, and the final standard was issued in 2009. The standard was a self-contained document without fallbacks to full IFRS. As a consequence, it was longer than had been hoped, since more topics had to be included.

Some people think the final standard is too complex. Among those entities interested to use it are, apparently, private subsidiaries of listed companies using IFRS, as well as private companies in the US where no small company version of US GAAP exists. The UK standard-setter is working on a plan to use the standard for larger private companies (i.e. with more than 50 employees) in place of UK GAAP. A European Commission consultation in 2010 showed that 19 EU member states supported the IFRS for SMEs, but six (including France, Germany and Italy) did not.

All of this tends to confirm that its rules are wide-ranging enough to meet the needs of reasonably sophisticated entities. However, a significant problem for countries where taxation is closely linked to financial reporting is that the IASB standard systematically sets aside both tax considerations and management information, as its Conceptual Framework requires, despite the fact that research generally shows that tax authorities and managers are two of the three most frequent users of SME accounts.

The IFRS for SMEs web pages noted (as at 1 August 2010) that 60 jurisdictions had adopted the standard, including Egypt, Malaysia, Hong Kong, Tanzania, Argentina, Brazil and the Philippines.

Content

The IASB restricts the use of the standard to 'non-publicly accountable' entities. This it defines as companies who do not have debt or equity

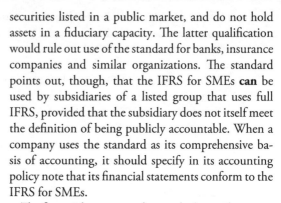

The IASB restricts the use of the standard to 'non-publicly accountable' entities

securities listed in a public market, and do not hold assets in a fiduciary capacity. The latter qualification would rule out use of the standard for banks, insurance companies and similar organizations. The standard points out, though, that the IFRS for SMEs **can** be used by subsidiaries of a listed group that uses full IFRS, provided that the subsidiary does not itself meet the definition of being publicly accountable. When a company uses the standard as its comprehensive basis of accounting, it should specify in its accounting policy note that its financial statements conform to the IFRS for SMEs.

The financial statements have to be 'general purpose financial statements' that are issued for the benefit of external users. The examples of external users are owners 'who are not involved in the management' and existing and potential creditors. The objective of the financial statement is to 'provide information about the financial position, performance and cash flows of the entity that is useful for economic decision-making by a broad range of users who are not in a position to demand reports tailored to meet their particular information needs'. The second objective is to 'show the results of the stewardship of management – the accountability of management for the resources entrusted to it'.

The technical content of the standard is summarized in Table 6.

The main features of the IFRS for SMEs are that it has simplified accounting for financial instruments. It classifies financial assets into only two categories, which was a simplification from the four categories of IAS 39, even if IFRS 9, the replacement of IAS 39 has also gone to two categories. In addition its hedge accounting and derecognition rules are simplified.

After much argument, the IASB also agreed that goodwill would be amortized over its useful life, with a 10-year maximum if its life was

Table 6 Contents: IFRS for SMEs

1	Small and Medium-sized Entities
2	Concepts and Pervasive Principles
3	Financial Statement Presentation
4	Statement of Financial Position
5	Statement of Comprehensive Income and Income Statement
6	Statement of Changes in Equity and Statement of Income and Retained Earnings
7	Statement of Cash Flows
8	Notes to the Financial Statements
9	Consolidated and Separate Financial Statements
10	Accounting Policies, Estimates and Errors
11	Basic Financial Instruments
12	Other Financial Instruments Issues
13	Inventories
14	Investments in Associates
15	Investments in Joint Ventures
16	Investment Property
17	Property, Plant and Equipment
18	Intangible Assets other than Goodwill
19	Business Combinations and Goodwill
20	Leases
21	Provisions and Contingencies Appendix — Guidance on recognizing and measuring provisions
22	Liabilities and Equity Appendix — Example of the issuer's accounting for convertible debt
23	Revenue Appendix — Examples of revenue recognition under the principles in Section 23
24	Government Grants
25	Borrowing Costs
26	Share-based Payment
27	Impairment of Assets
28	Employee Benefits
29	Income Tax
30	Foreign Currency Translation
31	Hyperinflation
32	Events after the End of the Reporting Period
33	Related Party Disclosures
34	Specialized Activities
35	Transition to the IFRS for SMEs

Source: IFRS Foundation.

unknown. Under full IFRS, goodwill is treated as having an indefinite life and is tested annually for impairment. IASB staff argued that having to conduct an impairment test was unduly expensive, and that lenders did not consider goodwill as an asset, so SMEs preferred to write off the intangible.

Other simplifications are that borrowing costs and development expenses are taken to profit and loss as incurred, whereas they must be capitalized under full IFRS. An SME is not required to review annually the carrying value of property, plant and equipment and the relevant depreciations schedules. It is required to review only when there is an indication that circumstances may have changed.

The IFRS for SMEs does not contain the full range of options that are available in full IFRS. In particular it does not offer the fair value option (to use fair value through profit and loss for assets or liabilities where otherwise there would be an accounting mismatch). Nor does it offer the revaluation alternative for property, plant and equipment. The standard omits altogether segment reporting, earnings per share, interim financial reporting and special treatment of assets held for sale. Disclosure requirements are considerably reduced.

Having sat through all the public meetings at which the IASB debated this standard, I would say that it represents a considerable achievement by Dr Pacter and the IASB staff. Certainly it is more complex than the UN Guideline, and perhaps more clearly oriented to the needs of developed counties than developing countries. However, starting from a position in 2003 where Board members were prepared to permit no changes from the recognition and measurement rules in full IFRS and few disclosure relaxations, the final standard is much simpler than one would have imagined it could be.

Conclusion

That the IASB should have produced a separate comprehensive basis of accounting for SMEs is quite surprising given its overt objective of writing high quality standards for capital markets, and the lack of evident experience in the SME world on the part of most Board members. However, there was political pressure to do this and sympathy on the part of the chairman and deputy chairman of the IASB. In effect they brought in a staff team from outside, which succeeded in producing a clear and credible document with some real concessions for SMEs even if the process took six years.

The IFRS for SMEs is now supported by extensive outreach activities to help countries adopt the standard and help individuals apply it, as well as to help teachers to train people. It has a support group, the SMEIG, which helps with application issues and with the regular update.

CHAPTER 8

COMPARISON WITH US GAAP

The aim of this chapter is to highlight some notable differences between US GAAP (the other most commonly found comprehensive basis of accounting in financial markets) and IFRS. It does not aim to be comprehensive. The first difference looked at is in the authoritative nature of their shared Conceptual Framework. Another major difference is in determining the scope of consolidation and interpreting the 'power' criterion. The chapter also looks at financial instruments, and related to that, offsetting of derivatives. It goes on to non-financial assets and impairment and a number of other differences.

Much of the first decade of the IASB's activities has been directed towards convergence with US GAAP. We will not know until the end of 2011 whether the US will adopt IFRS. If it does so, this will not take effect until 2014 or later, so US GAAP is not likely to disappear very soon. It seemed therefore potentially useful to review the major differences between IFRS and US GAAP as a guide to what work remains to be done if full convergence were to be reached, and as a guide to differences when both comprehensive bases of accounting exist along side each other.

Comparisons with US GAAP have been a bone of contention over many years. People who were against the use of international standards used to deploy such comparisons to show that US GAAP was much better. Supporters could argue that the differences might be many at a detailed level but were not that significant in terms of the actual numbers produced. During the 1990s the Financial Accounting Standards Board (FASB) widened its remit to include supporting the use of international standards and started to analyse International Accounting Standards (IAS).

Comparisons with US GAAP have been a bone of contention over many years

The FASB staff consequently monitored IAS and began to publish comparisons. The first detailed one was published in 1996 (*The IASC-US Comparison Project*, edited by Carrie Bloomer, FASB, Norwalk, Conn, USA). The rationale given for the comparison was that the International Organization of Securities Commissions was working with the IASC to develop reporting standards to be used internationally for secondary stock exchange listings (this subject is further developed in Chapter 11). The FASB said it wanted its constituents to be ready to analyse reports using IAS and also wanted to identify areas where work needed to be done for the IAS to be of the same standard as US GAAP.

The book identified 255 differences, which were split over different categories. The most critical category was the 56 cases where IAS required different accounting from US GAAP. There were 37 cases where US GAAP had rules but the IASC had issued none. Of course, not all these differences were desperately important, and their impact on financial statements was not necessarily material – but there were a lot of differences, given that these were both sets of standards that set out to report to investors in the Anglo-Saxon tradition.

Things have moved on a long way since then. The IASC issued a number of significant standards in the last part of the 1990s, including IAS 36 *Impairment of Assets*, IAS 38 *Intangible Assets* and IAS 39 *Financial Instruments: Recognition and Measurement*. The IASB took over in 2001 and started on a programme of convergence with US GAAP that involved one joint meeting a year at that point, and grew to the point in 2010 of meeting together every month, by video-link or in person. In 2002 the two Boards signed the 'Norwalk Agreement' that set out a programme of convergence. This had two main strands: the development of joint new standards (such as leases and revenue recognition) and convergence on the more modern existing standard when one standard-setter had recently revised its literature. An example is IFRS 8 *Operating Segments*, which aligned IFRS with the more recent US standard on segment reporting.

Since then, the two Boards signed a Memorandum of Understanding in 2006, which identified priorities in convergence work, and this was updated in 2008. The Securities and Exchange Commission (SEC) agreed in 2007 to recognize IFRS as issued by the IASB as equivalent to US GAAP for reporting by non-US companies that were registered with the SEC. This was a major milestone in convergence, and this was what had been envisaged by the FASB in the 1990s. Nonetheless the SEC and FASB were prepared to press on and see IFRS eventually become the single worldwide basis of accounting. This was reinforced by the G20 leaders in 2008 at their Pittsburgh summit when they called for the IASB and FASB to converge their standards.

It can be seen that the differences between the two sets of standards have become significant at a governmental level. Of course, they have been 'political' in a broader sense since the 1990s when many people would have preferred to use only US GAAP for reporting to the international capital markets. It can also be seen that those differences are in effect a moving target as both standard-setters move on, mostly reducing the differences but sometimes creating new ones.

It may be useful to contrast two slightly different views of what 'convergence' means. As we have talked about it above, it means standard-setters changing their standards to work towards a single set of standards. This is the sense that people have understood the word for the first decade of the IASB – largely convergence with US GAAP. However, there is a second use, which the SEC staff are starting to refer to, and this is convergence in the Chinese or Japanese sense. This means the process whereby a standard-setter decides to retain their own standards but move them as close as possible to IFRS. China has done this, and Japan started out on a programme of doing this, although it currently permits voluntary use of IFRS by listed companies, and may eventually adopt IFRS.

In the US context the discussion has tended to be whether or not the SEC should adopt IFRS. But in a document published in October 2010, the SEC staff pointed out that convergence in the Chinese or Japanese sense was also a possibility. In this chapter we are still talking about convergence in the sense of trying to build a common set of high quality standards, in other words, as envisaged in the Norwalk Agreement.

Conceptual Framework

One of the most fundamental differences between the two comprehensive bases of accounting is the role of the Conceptual Framework. As discussed earlier, their frameworks are very close and they are progressively moving towards a joint framework. However, in the US the role of the framework is to help the standard-setters set consistent standards, whereas for the IASB the framework plays that role but is also to be used by preparers and auditors to guide them in shaping an accounting policy when none exists in the standards.

The Conceptual Framework originated in the US and came out of a process of reform that was based in part on a perception that standards were inconsistent and were framed to help the audit firms. Up until 1973 standard-setting in the US was done by the overall professional body, the American Institute of Certified Public Accountants. Accounting scandals in the late 1960s led to a call for reform and the production of better standards. The answer was thought to be the creation of an independent standard-setter (the FASB) and a requirement that it should write standards that were consistent with an as yet only sketched out conceptual framework.

One of the most fundamental differences between the two comprehensive bases of accounting is the role of the Conceptual Framework

The FASB framework was elaborated from those reforms but as an instrument to serve only standard-setters who would write standards that gave effect to the objectives, etc., of the framework. Preparers and auditors would follow the standards. In the last few years the FASB has changed the way it structures its literature by amalgamating all the authoritative literature into the Accounting Standards Codification. Given its convergence with the IASB it did consider including the framework within that Codification, but eventually did not do so. Consequently, even the converged framework remains outside the US authoritative literature.

Under IFRS, however, the framework plays a second crucial role. It is intended to be used by companies as a guide when creating an accounting policy for which there is no direct guidance in the literature. Gilbert Gélard, a member of the IASB from 2001 to 2010, maintains that this aspect is essential in the context where IFRS aim to set principles and give limited guidance. He suggests that the company will frequently find itself confronted by situations where there is no guidance, and must develop its own accounting policy in compliance with the framework.

An extreme case of this might be the current revenue recognition project. Sir David Tweedie commented in a public meeting in 2010 that the US had 200 pieces of literature on revenue recognition, while IFRS had two standards (and references in three others). The company using IFRS should rely on the framework when there is no detailed guidance. I am not aware of any research evidence as to whether they actually do. The Big Four audit firms all produce large books of application guidance, and preparers could also look there, relying on the auditors to have consulted the Conceptual Framework on their behalf, perhaps.

Consolidation

The difference in consolidation approach between IFRS and US GAAP is a notorious one that is often cited as an example of the US preference for 'bright line' rules rather than professional judgement. The US requirement is based on a 1959 accounting standard which says that you must consolidate all companies that you control, and goes on to say that if you own more than 50% of the shares, then you **must** consolidate. This rule was written in a context of people trying not to consolidate companies where they owned more than 50% of the shares and does not rule out that you could control with less than 50% of the votes. However, practice established the 50% ownership as a bright line and all subsequent attempts by the FASB to move to a more judgemental approach have failed. A new attempt was made between 2009 and 2011 to introduce the IASB control notion without the 50% bright line. However, US respondents objected to this, saying that instances of control with less than 50% of the votes and without any supporting contractual framework did not exist in the UK. This therefore remains a difference.

Against this, the international standard (IAS 27 *Consolidated and Separate Financial Statements*, soon to be replaced with a new standard, IFRS 10) talks about control as the ability to affect the financial and operating decisions of the investee company. One could add that the European Seventh Company Law Directive (1983) is also based on the notion of economic control not necessarily legal control as determining what companies are fully consolidated. Clearly the effect of this underlying difference is that more companies should be consolidated by groups using IFRS than US GAAP.

When the French group Vivendi was being pursued by investors in the courts in New York (2009–2010), one of the issues was that it had consolidated SFR, the French telecoms company, in which it had a 40% stake at the time. Plaintiffs complained that SFR should not have been consolidated and in doing so the Vivendi group's cash resources were overstated.

However, the differences are probably more significant in relation to off balance sheet financing vehicles. The IASB has an Interpretation (SIC 12 *Consolidation – Special Purpose Entities*) that addresses this problem. The Interpretation says that when the substance of the relationship indicates that the investor controls the investee, the latter should be consolidated. The FASB has a difficult history in this area, where Enron, for one, used a bright line rule not to consolidate investee companies that it clearly controlled.

Since Enron, the FASB has concentrated its efforts on addressing special purpose entities rather than consolidation as a whole. It introduced the notion of the variable interest entity and concentrated more on issues such as who gets the main benefit from an entity, or who gets control if things go wrong (what standard-setters would call a 'risks and rewards' approach). However, this has been a fertile area for corporate banks and others to find 'structuring opportunities' to move debt outside of the consolidated group.

Financial instruments

This area is subject to so much pressure for change that it is almost not worth talking about. Both standard-setters are in the process of moving to a new model, and there is a lot of pressure for it to be a converged model, but it is too early yet to say if they will get there. Historically, the original IASB standard, IAS 39 *Financial Instruments: Recognition and Measurement*, was much influenced by US thinking, but as is often the case, if the basic approach was the same, the details often varied.

The US and international standards had the same categories of financial instruments, and broadly similar treatment for gains and losses. However, in 2003 the IASB introduced an option to value anything at fair value to correct an accounting mismatch (e.g. assets held at historical cost backing liabilities at fair value). The FASB subsequently also introduced a fair value option but with far fewer constraints.

Where there were possibly significant differences was impairment. The US had the concept of 'temporary impairment' and only assets that were other than temporarily impaired had to make a write-down. That write-down, however, was permanent, whereas under IAS 39 while write-downs must be made whenever there was an impairment, temporary or not, some could be reversed subsequently. In limited circumstances the FASB permitted reclassification whereas the IASB prohibited that until pressured by the European Union to make a relaxation in October 2008.

At the time of writing the situation is, to say the least, in a state of flux

At the time of writing the situation is, to say the least, in a state of flux. The IASB issued IFRS 9 *Financial Instruments* at the end of 2009. This dealt only with financial assets but financial liabilities have since been added. The standard can be adopted early but its probable obligatory application date is 1 January 2015. The standard will replace IAS 39 and will progressively have derecognition, hedging and impairment added to it before the application date. IFRS 9 introduces a two set classification system, with loans held for their underlying cash flows in one set accounting for at historical cost and everything else in another at fair value. It is intended to simplify and to add more practical rules on hedging and impairment.

However, the FASB has taken a divergent route. It issued an exposure draft in May 2010 which proposed the use of fair value for all financial instruments, although it too classifies instruments into two buckets. This has been greeted with less than enthusiasm by the Financial Stability Board, an organization closely linked to the Basel Committee of bank supervisors that has been charged by the G20 leaders with overseeing reform of the financial system.

In their report to the Seoul meeting of the G20 (10–12 November 2010), the FSB said the following:

In recommending to the Pittsburgh Summit that the IASB and FASB develop improved converged standards that would simplify and improve the accounting principles for financial instruments and their valuation, the FSB noted that it was particularly supportive of standards that would not expand the use of fair value in relation to the lending activities (involving loans and investments in debt instruments) of financial intermediaries. The IASB issued IFRS 9 in November 2009 which includes an amortized cost category for financial assets such as loans and certain investments in debt securities.

However, there is a potential for divergent accounting standards for lending activities, a subject of importance for financial stability, due to a FASB proposal in May 2010 to use fair value measurement on the balance sheet and through 'other comprehensive income' for loans and investments in debt securities. Under this proposal, changes in fair values of lending instruments would affect reported shareholders' equity, but generally would not be included in profit and loss. In response to FASB's request for feedback from interested parties on the ED, and based upon extensive outreach by the FASB, it appears that the majority of investors and other stakeholders do not agree with the fair value measurement recognition aspects of this proposal as it relates to lending activities, deposits, and other liabilities. The FSB welcomes the enhanced outreach and hopes that the accounting boards' consideration of stakeholders' comments will result in improved and converged approaches in their final standards. The FSB encourages the IASB and FASB to continue their efforts to achieve improved converged financial instrument accounting standards by June 2011.

(Source: *Progress since the Washington Summit in the Implementation of the G20 Recommendations for Strengthening Financial Stability: Report of the Financial Stability Board to G20 Leaders Financial Stability Board*, Basel, 8 November 2010, p.16.)

The US is under pressure to change and the likelihood is that the two standard-setters will have a more converged approach by the end of 2011. For the moment they have similar but different standards in force, but the situation will change over the short to medium term to classification into two categories.

Offsetting

Linked to financial instruments is the issue of offsetting, or netting. This is a presentation issue and involves presenting the net amount due under two opposite contracts. For example, if you were a builder who owed a car dealer €30,000 for the purchase of a truck, but the dealer owed you €20,000 for building a showroom, you have opposite contracts, and you might want to show in your balance sheet a net payable of €10,000, instead of a payable of €30,000 and a receivable of €20,000.

This is not usually a particularly significant issue for non-financial businesses, but it can be very significant for financial institutions that may have very many contracts in both directions with other financial institutions. At the moment the IFRS rules differ from those of the US, and non-US banks appear to have much larger balance sheets than their US counterparts, because the US banks are able to offset more widely.

The subject is dealt with in IAS 1 *Presentation of Financial Statements*, which carries a general prohibition of offsetting, except where another standard allows it in particular circumstances. IAS 32 *Financial*

Instruments: Presentation makes such an exception. It allows assets and liabilities with the same counterparty to be offset in the financial statements (not in the accounting books) where (a) there is a legal and enforceable right to offset, and (b) the entity has the intention to pay net or make simultaneous settlement.

US GAAP, however, is less restrictive when it comes to derivatives and contracts exchanged under a Master Netting Agreement (MNA). The MNA is a standard kind of contract used in the developed financial markets that is put in place between two contracting parties and all contracts issued between the two are issued under this umbrella arrangement. MNAs are not all exactly the same, but the main point of them is that in the event of default, all the contracts are frozen and a net amount is calculated. US GAAP has the same basic prohibitions as IFRS but makes an exception for contracts exchanged under an MNA. This means that a bank with a significant activity in derivatives does not on the face of the financial statements disclose the full extent of their liabilities nor the full extent of their assets.

In discussing whether the IASB might move to this, the point was made that under an MNA, the contracts do not have the same settlement dates nor necessarily the same currency, etc., so they are not normally offsettable. They only become offsettable when the series of exchanges is brought to a halt by default, at which point all the contracts become immediately due for settlement. The difference in approaches has been raised by the Financial Stability Board as an issue to be resolved. The FASB and IASB issued an exposure draft in January 2011 proposing to converge their requirements on lines close to the IAS 32 requirements.

Non-financial assets

One of the better-known differences between US GAAP and IFRS concerns research and development. The US takes the view that all such expenditure should be expensed as incurred, whereas IAS 38 *Intangible Assets* requires that pure research expenditure be expensed but development costs must be capitalized. The development costs are those incurred after the entity has identified a viable product and determined that it can be manufactured, is likely to be profitable, and the company has the resources to develop it successfully.

The advantages of the one approach against the other are open to debate. On the one hand there is an inconsistency with all internally generated intangibles, that they are not typically capitalized while purchased intangibles will appear in the balance sheet. There is also the conceptual argument that the conditions surrounding development expenditure mean that such expenditure meets the definition of an asset – the company controls the output and expects to generate future cash flows. One could argue that the FASB position contravenes the Conceptual Framework. On the other hand, expensing these items at once is more efficient from a tax perspective.

One of the better-known differences between US GAAP and IFRS concerns research and development

IAS 38 has both a cost model and a revaluation model. Under the cost model, intangibles are amortized over their expected economic life. Where they have an indefinite life they are not amortized but are tested for impairment. The standard allows of the possibility of holding an intangible at valuation; however, it also states (IAS 38.78) that this is only possible where there is an active market for this type of intangible. The paragraph adds that such markets are rare because of the individual nature of most intangibles, and cannot exist for 'brands, newspaper mastheads, music and film publishing rights, patents or trademarks, because each such asset is unique'.

Investment property is another fairly major difference. US GAAP does not provide any special accounting for investment property, and it is accounted for at amortized cost. However, IAS 40 *Investment Property* identifies this special class as:

property (land or a building – or part of a building – or both) held (by the owner or by the lessee under a finance lease) to earn rentals or for capital appreciation or both, rather than for:

(a) use in the production or supply of goods or services or for administrative purposes; or

(b) sale in the ordinary course of business.

Such property is recognized initially at cost, but subsequent measurement may be under the cost model or using fair value. Under the latter the property is carried at balance sheet date at its market price at balance sheet date. The fair value gain or loss is taken to profit and loss. The FASB has expressed some interest in developing its own version of this, but generally historical cost is the rule for non-financial assets.

IAS 16 *Property, Plant and Equipment* is the general international standard for tangible non-current assets. Aside from historical cost, the standard also permits valuation as an alternative measurement basis. This not much used but offers a possible line of defence in economies where there is significant inflation. However, the standard requires a programme of continuing valuation, which can be quite expensive in terms of professional fees to valuers.

Another significant difference is that IAS 16 has a 'components' approach to accounting for tangible assets and depreciating them. The components approach means that companies are required to identify significant elements of a composite asset that have different economic lives. As an example the lifts, central heating and air conditioning plant in an office block should be separately identified from the building itself and potentially be depreciated over a different life.

Impairment

This is another of those areas where the two comprehensive bases of accounting are fairly similar, but the practical detail differs in some ways that may on occasion be significant. IAS 36 *Impairment* requires that goodwill and intangible assets with an indefinite life should be tested at each balance sheet date for impairment, but other assets are tested only if there is some indication that impairment may have taken place. The impairment test involves comparing the 'recoverable amount' (the higher of either the fair value less costs to sell or the present value of expected future cash flows) with the carrying amount and writing down the carrying amount if it is above the recoverable amount. Once goodwill is impaired, the impairment cannot be reversed, but other impairments can be cancelled if the situation improves subsequently.

This compares with the general position of US GAAP, which is a two-step process. The carrying amount is compared with the present value of the expected future cash flows. If the carrying amount is higher, the asset is written down to fair value. Impairments cannot be reversed.

Linked to impairment is the notion of the Cash Generating Unit (CGU). Under IFRS this is the smallest unit that is capable of generating cash flows independently of the rest of the group. Impairment under IFRS is done at the CGU level. Where a CGU has been acquired as part of the acquisition of another company, the acquiring company is required to allocate goodwill down to the CGU level, and apply the impairment provision first to goodwill and then proportionately to other non-current assets. US GAAP also has the CGU notion, but it is defined at a higher level, generally a business unit at one level below the segment. The implication is that under IFRS you would be likely to recognize impairment more often, because with the smaller CGU there is less opportunity for profitable operations to be pooled with unprofitable.

Miscellaneous

Another of the better known differences between US GAAP and IFRS is the use of Last In First Out (LIFO) as a measurement basis for inventory. Although under US tax law what is in the financial statements is not generally determining in terms of taxable income, a major exception is that if an entity wants to use LIFO for tax purposes, it must also do so for financial reporting purposes. As a consequence a number of manufacturing companies in the US do use LIFO. However, it is not permitted under IAS 2 *Inventories*. The international standard only allows First In First Out (FIFO) and weighted average cost.

Deferred taxation is an area that used to cause problems for companies using IFRS that were registered with the SEC when reconciling their profits to US GAAP. Although both sets of standards apply the basic principle of recognizing deferred tax on any difference between the carrying value of an asset and its tax value, they both have complex exceptions that result in their giving different results for the same situation. US rules, of course, reflect US tax requirements, where IAS 12 has to stand outside any legal framework.

The IASB and FASB have made heroic attempts to converge their tax standards but the outcome has been just the consumption of a lot of staff and board time with no progress. One area where they differ is in the recognition of future tax rates. IAS 12 says you reflect future rates when they become reasonably certain, whereas in the US you only recognize them when the President has signed the tax legislation. In many jurisdictions, when the government of the day announces its future intentions, the rates of tax announced can be taken to be reasonably certain. However, given the nature of the US political system, the same is not true there.

> *The IASB and FASB have made heroic attempts to converge their tax standards*

An issue related to that is that the US allows companies to shelter overseas profits in offshore companies under some circumstances. If they repatriate the profits, though, they become subject to US tax. US GAAP does not require the catch-up tax to be reflected in the financial statements ahead of return to the US. Some people argue that this means that cash positions are overstated and tax understated since if a group wants to repatriate the cash held offshore it would have to pay another 25–30% taxation.

So far IFRS does not have a standard that looks at the special assets and liabilities of rate-regulated industries. This is a problem for Canada, as it adopts in 2011, and is a significant difference with the US. For those not familiar with the issue, in some countries services such as electricity and water are provided by private sector entities, which are subject to the control of a public regulator – particularly as to what price they can charge (hence 'rate-regulated'). The aim is to allow the supplier to recover their legitimate costs plus an appropriate return on capital.

However, in practice there is a regular need to fine tune and the supplier sometimes recovers too much, sometimes too little. When this happens the regulator adjusts the price in a future period to compensate. Where the supplier has made too much money, they would normally recognize a liability that will be satisfied against lower prices in the future. Equally, if the supplier does not make enough, they recognize an asset representing the right to future revenue. Such entities consequently recognize a special type of asset and liability that does not occur in other industries.

The IASB has, at Canada's request, considered writing a standard to enable recognition of such assets and liabilities. However there was a lot of opposition to this and the subject is in abeyance for the moment. Some people think that regulatory assets and liabilities do not meet the Conceptual Framework definitions. This has not been a concern shared by the FASB whose standards address rate-regulated industries.

The IASB is well on the way towards producing a final standard on insurance contracts. The US has its own insurance standards, which are not the same. Among other things, the US has different rules for different types of insurance. It is possible, but far from certain, that the FASB will converge on the IFRS. The IASB is committed to issuing its final standard by June 2011, and may well create divergence by doing so.

A subtle difference between the US and IFRS is the meaning of the word 'probable'. Under IFRS, probable means 'more likely than not' – so just over 50% likely. However in FASB usage, probable means almost certain – maybe 75% or 80% likely. This subtle distinction illustrates that two standard-setters can use the same words in the same language and still mean something different.

Conclusion

In this chapter we have aimed to bring together some of the main differences between US GAAP and IFRS. They are mentioned where appropriate in the text elsewhere, but this chapter may be useful to people who work with both comprehensive bases of accounting. We would underline that the spirit of convergence would suggest that these differences will disappear over time.

CHAPTER 9

THE IASB'S STANDARD-SETTING PROCESS

This chapter provides a detailed analysis of the standard-setting process. It aims to show all of the stages in the writing of a standard and explain how the constituent can interact with the standard-setter and help shape the standard in some way. The chapter also discusses the organizational structure and the functions of the various committees that operate together under the aegis of the IFRS Foundation.

This chapter looks at how the IASB sets standards, at what points the standard-setters consult their constituents, and how you can influence their standard-setting. You may wonder if you need to know this – in fact not, if all you are interested in doing is applying IFRS or reading financial statements that are based on IFRS. However, a little knowledge of the process will help you understand the context when you may read a report about an 'exposure draft' being issued or something like that. Finally, you may want to engage much more closely with the system, keep well informed on what the IASB is doing and be aware what changes are coming down the line. In that case you should read this chapter attentively!

One of the marked differences in national standard-setting systems is the extent to which accounting standards are actually part of statute law, and the legal authority of the standard-setter. In anglophone countries there is a tradition of standard-setting being done by technical experts within a general framework provided by the law. In the US, for example, US standards are written by the Financial Accounting Standards Board (FASB), but this is within a framework where the legal responsibility lies with the Securities and Exchange Commission (SEC) which can, and does, override the FASB's pronouncements. This contrasts with the French system where since the 1940s the standard-setter has been part of the Ministry of Finance.

The IASB ... exists outside of any national framework and there is no international statute law

In the French case, the legitimacy of the standards is established by the governmental nature of the standard-setter, and in recent years, by each standard being issued under a government order. In the US case, the legitimacy of the standards is supported by seeking a consensus with constituents and inviting their input to the process. In the French case, standard-setting takes place usually behind closed doors, whereas in the US case, it is done in public ('in the sunshine'). Draft documents are published to allow constituents to comment on the proposals, which are often modified in the light of this exposure process. A French auditor or preparer doesn't necessarily expect to know much about the standards in preparation, while a US constituent expects to hear a lot about what the FASB is doing!

The IASB, of course, is a special case because, being international, it exists outside of any national framework and there is no international statute law. In any event, it is a standard-setter in the anglophone tradition – the standard-setters are accounting experts, not politicians, even if in some countries (and the European Union) its standards are translated into national law before being applied by constituents. Arguably, as an international standard-setter, free of any direct governmental oversight, it has an even greater need to seek legitimacy and authority through extensive consultation. The IASB does have an oversight system of governance, but we will address that later in the chapter, first we will look at the consultation process, known as 'due process'.

Due process

The IASB's due process has become more elaborate over time, and is now enshrined in a document (*IASB Due Process Handbook*) that can be consulted from the website. The process consists of a series of stages:

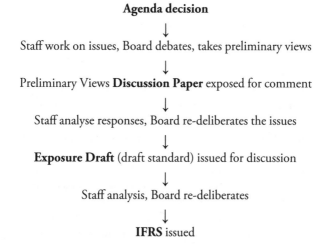

Agenda decision

↓

Staff work on issues, Board debates, takes preliminary views

↓

Preliminary Views **Discussion Paper** exposed for comment

↓

Staff analyse responses, Board re-deliberates the issues

↓

Exposure Draft (draft standard) issued for discussion

↓

Staff analysis, Board re-deliberates

↓

IFRS issued

For some reason, agenda decisions are a political hot potato. Some constituents get very excited about how a decision is made to deal with one subject and not another. In fact there is a formal process. The IASB has criteria that have to be met for an item to be considered. Various organizations make informal suggestions, but usually the problem is trying to sort out what topics should be at the top of the priority list and the IASB consults widely on this.

Having identified something that is thought to be a priority, staff have to prepare an agenda decision paper. This analyses the accounting issue, explains why people think there is a problem, and considers whether the issue meets the necessary criteria. This paper is formally reviewed by an advisory body (the IFRS Advisory Council) and the oversight body (Trustees of the IFRS Foundation). If they are in agreement, then the paper is formally put to the Board.

This should be the start of work on the topic, but in practice even when an item is on the formal agenda it can get sidelined, either because there is a lack of enthusiasm (e.g. intangible assets) or there are more pressing priorities (the financial crisis pushed aside consideration of issues such as emissions allowances, and the extractive industry). An item may be sidelined formally by being transferred to the 'research agenda', or informally by no project team being assigned and no Board time allocated.

Work on preparing standards is done by the IASB's extensive full-time technical staff. The basic model is that staff write technical papers and make recommendations that are then debated by the IASB at its monthly public standard-setting meeting. However, some subjects are more complex than others, and some are more difficult to resolve, and the arrangements can be modified depending on the nature of the project. With a major project such as financial instruments, the IASB will assemble an advisory group of experts in the area concerned. This acts as a sounding board for the staff and enables them to get continuous feedback and information as they work on the subject. Usually the IASB also appoints 'Board advisors' – one or two individual Board members are assigned the task of discussing ongoing work on a project with the staff.

Discussion paper

Work proceeds on an iterative basis: staff write a paper that addresses part of the problem and the possible solutions to that. They take it to the Board and get feedback as well as 'tentative decisions' and then move on to another part. Over time this will lead to a complete preliminary views discussion paper. The draft paper, which will usually take about a year and a half to prepare (more for a controversial topic), will be the subject of a secret written ballot by Board members. Only a simple majority of votes is required for issue.

The Board believes that it is better to issue a 'preliminary views' paper that tells constituents clearly the direction of the Board's preferences, rather than a discussion paper that just sets out the alternatives. Nonetheless, a preliminary views paper will normally include a discussion of alternative approaches and explain why the Board prefers one against another. It is not, however, unknown for constituents to reject the Board's proposals, and for the Board to think again. The Board's 2008 preliminary views paper on derecognition of financial assets proposed one model but gave details of another that the Board had rejected. Constituents said they preferred the rejected model, so the Board thought again.

in practice discussion papers are not always translated

The discussion document is published in English and will be left open for comment, usually for four months, but longer if the Board considers the topic difficult, or if its publication comes around a financial year-end when most constituents are very busy. This is notionally one month for translation and three months for comment, although in practice discussion papers are not always translated, and most people close to the process use English as a working language.

The IASB has the constitutional freedom to vary this part of the process quite a lot. There is no **requirement** to issue a discussion paper, and the IASB does not always do so. However, it has come to be recognized by the IFRS community that there is most opportunity to involve constituents when there is a discussion paper stage. Board members feel free to expose alternative approaches whereas the Exposure Draft is a draft regulation. Consequently the IASB's practice is to issue a discussion document on all major projects.

The IASB may also decide to invite additional contact with constituents. Sometimes after publication of a discussion paper the IASB will hold round tables in different parts of the world. Typically it invites people who have sent in formal comment letters to attend a round table discussion where they can talk to each other, and staff and Board members can ask questions to attempt to flesh out different aspects of constituents' reactions.

In recent times the staff have also conducted outreach programmes during the process of working on standards to check individual points directly with constituents. This has been done extensively during work on financial crisis projects and seems to have worked well. Constituents appear to be better informed of the direction the Board is taking, and at the same time the Board gets regular feedback, which avoids the potential for going out with a proposal that is judged unworkable at a practical level. The only concern voiced so far about this process is that the choice of constituents with whom to do outreach is not transparent. However, the likelihood is that anyone with a strong interest in a particular topic would be listened to by staff if they made contact.

Exposure draft

Once the exposure period has ended, the staff begin the process of analysing the responses to the discussion paper. These responses are published on the IASB's website, so constituents can access them. The Board will normally get at least a hundred comment letters after publishing a discussion document, but it could be twice that number if the subject is controversial. However, the number is sometimes exaggerated when members of an interest group write in separately. For example, when the IASB was looking at share-based payment, about 80 members of Financial Executives International sent in the same form letter. When the project is being run jointly with the FASB, both standard-setters may issue the same paper and then share comment letters.

Usually the first thing that the staff do is bring to the Board an agenda paper that provides an overview of the comments. This can be accessed either from the project page or from the meetings diary – but you need to research the date on which the item was debated. The paper will analyse the type of respondent (e.g. national standard-setters, audit firms, professional associations, etc.) and the nature of their comments. Some constituents respond systematically to all documents published for comment, while others write only if the issue directly concerns them. On the whole the staff are careful to avoid talking about numbers – they should not say 'the majority of respondents approve …', for example, because the respondents might be individuals or large organizations.

The staff will next start to re-deliberate all the issues in the discussion paper, asking the Board to confirm its preliminary view, or suggesting that it modifies its view. A considerable amount of opposition to a proposal will not necessarily mean that the staff will advise a change of position. They will evaluate from whom the opposition comes, and what is the basis of it. Historically, preparers of financial reports will nearly always only bother to write if they **oppose** a proposal, and in any event, the standard-setter is looking at providing information that helps users, not preparers.

If a preparer objects, they need to advance arguments that the information is not useful to users, or that it is costly or impractical to provide the information. Often, however, preparers say their business will disappear or some other variant on 'the world will come to an end if …'. Unfortunately, standard-setters are unlikely to be convinced by such an argument because past experience suggests the prediction is not accurate.[1] If users say the information is not useful, though, this may well prove fatal to the proposal. Auditors sometimes take a view on how feasible it is to audit the information, or may take a view about what approach provides better information.

Some authors suggest that the point of due process is to reach a consensus, and then claim that the IASB is not following due process when it fails to change a position that many people oppose. This is a little naïve – the IASB is aiming to improve the quality of financial reporting in terms of how it informs investor decision-making. It does not expect that even all users will agree on that, let alone preparers and auditors.

The project will go through a complete re-debate of all the salient points until the staff reach a situation where they believe they are ready to draft the exposure draft. They ask Board permission to go ahead with this and also ask if any Board member is likely to dissent. An exposure draft needs nine votes out of 15 in favour before it can be issued (10 votes out of 16 when the Board size is increased). If a Board member plans to vote against it, they are required to publish details of why they disagree as part of the exposure draft. Most exposure drafts include one or more dissenting opinions, but some Board members are more likely to dissent than others. Jim Leisenring, who retired from the IASB in 2010, was well known for his dissents.

Once the draft has been written, it is circulated privately to Board members as a 'pre-ballot draft' and they are asked to raise any issues. The IASB refers to these as 'sweep issues'. They may just concern wording that a member does not like, but are sometimes disagreements that the Board actually agreed to what the staff say they did. Once these

---

1 I was amused when observing a meeting between the IASB and EFRAG to hear Sir David Tweedie use a similar argument about US adoption of IFRS. He said in effect worldwide convergence would come to an end if the US did not adopt. He presumably was not conscious of the parallel.

matters have been dealt with, the Board takes a secret ballot, and the exposure draft is published.

The exposure draft will also include a 'Basis for Conclusions' in which the staff set out the reasons why the Board rejected particular alternatives from among those available. For the lobbyist the Basis for Conclusions is an interesting document, although it may not include **all** of the reasons that were mentioned in debate. The exposure draft may also include guidance as to how to implement the proposals. These will also appear in the final standard.

For the lobbyist the Basis for Conclusions is an interesting document

New standard

The staff and Board follow pretty well the same process for the comments on the exposure draft as for the discussion paper. There are, though, some subtle differences in approach. In effect while the discussion paper is showing different possibilities, the exposure draft is saying: 'OK, we have considered the possibilities, and this is our decision'. Consequently the Board is not looking for feedback on different approaches, but is rather giving constituents the opportunity to point out 'fatal flaws' in the proposal. Many respondents will, of course, still write in saying they prefer an alternative model, but unless they can advance some arguments that were not brought up at discussion paper stage, the Board is likely just to confirm its earlier decisions.

The main area for any flexibility between exposure draft and final standard is on the toughness of the standard. Due process requires that the final standard should not include any requirement that has not been exposed for comment. This means that if in re-debating the exposure draft position the Board decides to change something substantive, the proposal has to be re-exposed. Members prefer to avoid that if at all possible because it potentially delays the whole project by a further year (equally lobbyists against a proposal prefer to ask for re-exposure to delay implementation). As a consequence, the Board will tend to put tougher requirements in the exposure draft than it necessarily wants, so that it retains the possibility of imposing them , but may also pull back in the final standard..

This is particularly true of things like disclosure requirements. For example, the staff may ask for an analysis of all changes in a balance sheet line item over the reporting period (a 'roll-forward' schedule), but the Board would actually be willing to settle just for a breakdown of the main components at the year-end. The exposure draft will ask for the full analysis so that that possibility remains open without re-exposure. It is therefore worth lobbying for a reduction of severity, even if arguing for a change in model is probably a waste of effort.

The final standard will include transitional arrangements. These are often quite complicated. In principle IAS 8 says that all new standards should be applied retrospectively – i.e. as if they had always been in force. However, this is rarely possible, partly because the entity might not have the information available to re-state past transactions, and partly because retrospective application may imply the use of hindsight in making valuations. The IASB is systematically against the use of hindsight, especially if fair value is concerned. Consequently the transitional arrangements will attempt to find a path that gets to comparable treatments as quickly as possible, but within these constraints.

The standard will include an 'effective date' – the date at which application of the standard becomes obligatory. This is always a year or more after the date the standard is issued, and usually starts on 1 January or 1 July. The year's delay is to allow time for the standard to be translated from English and also for it to be enacted into national or regional law if that is necessary (as is the case in the European Union).

In addition, however, the IASB takes note of external circumstances and voluntarily sets 'stand-still' periods where no new standards are brought into force. It did this in 2005, when the EU and other jurisdictions moved to IFRS, guaranteeing that while it would work on new standards, none would have an effective date before 2009. This gave companies time to let the systems settle in before tinkering with them. It has also done this for the period following 2011 when a significant number of countries will start to use IFRS.

In these circumstances, the IASB will, however, allow early adoption. That is, entities may choose to apply the standards before their official effective date (if their jurisdiction allows that). Board members argue that if they have issued a new standard, it is implicit that they think this incorporates better information, so why would they want to prevent people providing better information if they wanted to? Against that, users complain that allowing early adoption leads to lack of comparability between companies.

Another detail is that the new standard will usually incorporate any Interpretations that address the same subject, and these will disappear from the literature. For example, the new standard on consolidations incorporates and replaces both IAS 27, the previous standard, and SIC 12, the Interpretation that deals with special purpose entities.

Interpretations

It is actually quite easy to lose sight of Interpretations, even though they are just as much part of the authoritative literature as standards. Essentially the IFRS Interpretations Committee (previously known as the International Financial Reporting Interpretations Committee – IFRIC, which replaced the Standards Interpretations Committee) responds to queries on how to interpret standards. It is an unpaid committee, consisting of 14 people, mostly auditors and preparers, and it meets six times a year to discuss technical questions put to it. The questions often come from international audit firms, but might also come from national regulators or others: their origin is never revealed publicly. The Committee is supposed to provide an authoritative Interpretation, which is approved by the IASB. The Committee also deals with issues under the IASB's Annual Improvements Process.

In theory the IFRS Interpretations Committee cannot change the existing literature but is supposed to address questions where there is a possible conflict between standards, or there is confusion about what a standard means, or people want to know if a standard can be applied in circumstances other than those considered in the standard.

It is actually quite easy to lose sight of Interpretations

An example of an Interpretation is IFRIC 13 *Customer Loyalty Programmes*. Constituents noted that IAS 18 *Revenue* provided two possible treatments of 'free' gifts given to customers when they make a purchase, such as air miles granted with a ticket purchase. One treatment calls for the entity to accrue a liability for the cost of the subsequent gift, while recognizing all the revenue at once. The other treatment in the same standard suggests that the initial revenue should be split between the substantive purchase and the 'gift' with revenue for the initial purchase limited to a proportion of what was actually paid. While the choice does not affect profit, it does affect the timing of revenue recognition. IFRIC ruled that there was diversity in practice and only one method, the second one, was correct.

The due process for such problems is that the questions go to the staff who prepare an agenda paper for the Committee with a recommendation as to whether the Committee should address it. The criteria are that there is diversity in practice and that an Interpretation could be produced in a reasonable time to counter this diversity.

The Committee will then issue a draft agenda decision, which is published for comment for 30 days. Most agenda decisions are in fact negative: frequently the Committee says there is no need to issue an Interpretation, the standard is clear. In this case, the agenda decision itself will generally contain useful guidance, even if it is not authoritative. In other cases the Committee may decide that the standard needs changing, so an Interpretation is not useful, or the topic is so complex or controversial that no Interpretation could be issued within the Committee's time constraints.

If the Committee thinks the standard needs changing, the next step is to decide if this is simply an editorial amendment that is uncontroversial, or if it is more than that. An uncontroversial change in wording goes to the Annual Improvements Process – this is a system for dealing with straightforward improvements or clarifications in standards. It was instituted to avoid having multiple insignificant amendments going through on a month to month basis. Although this was originally handled by the IASB directly, this has passed to the Interpretations Committee, who debate possible amendments and then pass them to the IASB for approval. If a change is thought to be needed but is potentially controversial, it goes directly to the IASB, who may or may not accept to address it.

In the relatively few cases that are carried through to be dealt with as Interpretations, due process is much the same as for standards. The staff bring papers to the Committee and address the issues on which decisions are needed. Once a qualified majority approval has been given, the staff prepare a draft Interpretation. This is passed to the IASB for negative clearance (it is issued as long as no more than four members disagree) and published. After an exposure period (usually 60 days) it is brought back for re-discussion in the light of the comments. The version finally approved by the Committee then goes back to the IASB for formal approval.

It should be noted that Bob Garnett, the chairman of the Committee, was also a member of the IASB until June 2010. Some Board members attend meetings of the Committee and the senior staff member responsible for the Committee (the director of implementation activities) also gives the Board updates after every meeting. In theory Board members are aware on a continuing basis of what topics the Committee is addressing and the direction it is taking.

Structure

The chapter so far has given you the essentials of due process. This next section provides background detail on the structure of the organization (Figure 1).

While the heart of the organization is the IASB, the controlling body comprises the Trustees of the IFRS Foundation (formerly known as the IASC Foundation). The Trustees, who are 22 in number, are supposed to guarantee the independence of the IASB. The Trustees are also supposed to raise money for the organization and are responsible for appointing Board members, staff and members of the different advisory bodies. At the same time, the chairman of the IASB is also the chief executive of the IFRS Foundation, which gives that person a curious dual role as chief executive of his (or her) own supervisory body.

Since 2009 the Trustees themselves have had to answer to a Monitoring Board. The creation of the Monitoring Board was an answer to governance issues, as the Trustees were accused of being a self-

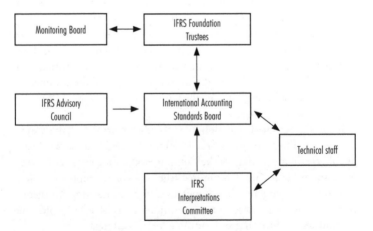

Figure 1 Structure of standard-setting organization.

perpetuating body that was accountable to no one (they decide on their own appointments as well as those of everyone else connected with the organization). The Monitoring Board consists of representatives of the European Union, the SEC, the Japanese Financial Services Agency and two representatives from the International Organization of Securities Commissions (representing worldwide capital markets).

The Monitoring Board has regular meetings with the Trustees and the Chief Executive to discuss Trustee decisions, especially concerning appointments. While the Monitoring Board does not itself make appointments it is thought to have been instrumental in the appointment of Hans Hoogervorst as chairman of the IASB from July 2011. Mr Hoogervorst has been a finance minister in the Dutch government and subsequently head of the Dutch securities regulator. He was also chairman of the Monitoring Board.

The arrangements between the Monitoring Board and the Trustees are unlikely to remain as they currently stand. Both the Monitoring Board and the Trustees launched consultations on the future governance of the IASB in 2010, which should lead to changes in 2011 or later. There are two significant problems: one is that the IASB is financed by largely voluntary payments solicited by the Trustees (see below), and the other is that countries that adopt IFRS have absolutely no voice in the governance of the standard-setter. The Trustees argue that their role and the reason for the structure is to protect the standard-setter from political or other influence. However it is not clear that they are successful in doing this, while it is clear that governments think the IASB should be accountable for its decisions.

The IFRS Advisory Council is the permanent body that is supposed to advise and comment on the IASB's work. It meets three times a year. However, the Foundation appoints many other special advisory groups to address particular issues. The exact nature of these groups can be seen by going to the IASB's website (www.iasb.org). At the time of writing the principal standing groups were the Financial Crisis Advisory Group, the Analyst Representative Group and the Global

Preparers Forum. In addition to these it had working groups related to particular projects, including insurance, financial instruments, employee benefits and financial statement presentation.

Finance

The funding of the IASB has always been a delicate issue. When it started it was funded by voluntary contributions, $1m each from the (then) Big Five international audit firms, as well as gifts of up to $50,000 from companies and contributions by regulators, banks and others. Some people did not like this on the basis that it meant the IASB was not independent of its donors, even though the IFRS Foundation was there to guarantee that. But at a practical level it was also not very comfortable, and so the Trustees have tried to move to a system where each economy provides a regular contribution.

The funding of the IASB has always been a delicate issue

This has not proved very easy either. While Germany and the UK have provided nearly €1m a year each, other countries such as France have been reluctant to contribute when they disagree with what the IASB is doing and did not want to have to use IFRS anyway. The European Commission has also provided funds since 2010, but this is likely to cause national contributions to be reduced accordingly while providing a pressure point for European interests.

The IASB needs about €25m a year to function. It continues to receive financial support from the Big Four international audit firms (now $2m a year each), from some mid-tier audit firms and from many institutions, but is now tending to spend more than it receives, particularly during the financial crisis, where it has had many extra standard-setting meetings, and many joint meetings with the FASB. The IASB's dependence on voluntary contributions has also been identified by the SEC as a significant issue in terms of possible US adoption of IFRS. The SEC thinks that the standard-setter should receive funds automatically. The FASB now is financed by a levy on companies registered with the SEC, even if for 25 years it was, like the IASB, funded by voluntary contributions.

In its first 10 years of operation the IASB made about a third of its revenue from the margin on publishing sales. It sells individual standards and an annual volume of standards and it also has an electronic updating service. Formally speaking, the electronic version of the standards is the authoritative source as to which standards are in force. The IASB's very complete electronic package includes internet access to all the literature as well as all sorts of updates about IASB activity. Authors must also pay the IASB to quote from its literature, so in buying this book you are indirectly contributing to the IASB's resources.

However, the IASB's ability to make money in this way is slightly constrained. On the one hand, the EU has to make available its literature free of charge to constituents, and since it formally endorses IFRS into EU law, you can download IFRS free of charge from the European Commission's website. On the other hand, the IASB has decided that it will in the future make the text of the actual standards available free of charge. However, the free version will not include the Basis for Conclusions nor guidance material.

Lobbying the IASB

As this chapter has discussed due process, it has also indicated where it is possible to contribute to the formation of a standard. In this section we will just go over the basics of that. Essentially, it is important to intervene as early as possible in the process to put forward your view. The first key stage is the agenda decision. If you were trying to avoid the IASB addressing a subject, the best thing you can do is lobby against including it on the agenda, if you know that this is a possibility.

How do you lobby? Well, so far the IASB is relatively open in terms of e-mail addresses being easily available, so you can correspond with the Technical Director or Board members. You can write to them to express a view, but probably it is more effective if you can send them research material that would help them in making a decision.

Once an item has gone on the active agenda, the next most fruitful approach is to offer to participate in the working group, if there is one. If there is no such group, you can still offer to assist the staff by giving access to your business, for example, so that they can see what the problems are in practice. Research material or factual analyses are also very useful. Staff and Board members in the first instance want to know as much as possible about the realities of the area they plan to work on before they start taking positions. So this is the time to establish a fruitful relationship by offering cooperation. In this way you will be closely in touch with developments. As the project proceeds, staff will start to bring agenda papers to the Board and you will need to study these closely and eventually comment on them yourself. The agenda papers can be downloaded from the meetings section of the website and often also from the relevant project page. The IASB's recent emphasis on outreach activities has made staff even more open to discussing projects with interested constituents.

A discussion paper will be issued, and this will probably look at more than one accounting model. If you have a preference, you should respond to the discussion paper and state your arguments formally for the record. If the Board decides to hold round tables or other direct consultations, you will probably be offered the opportunity to participate, once you have submitted a formal comment letter (but not if you have not submitted a comment letter).

The next stage, where the staff move the project from discussion paper to exposure draft, is the most critical one – decisions are taken that are rarely changed subsequently. Here again you need to stay close to the subject by reading the papers put to the Board, and also commenting directly to staff members and Board members. You will also get the chance to comment formally on the exposure draft, but while it is important to put your views officially on the record, the chances of changing anything at this stage are slim. Once again the Board will go through the process of re-debating the key issues, but although you will want to monitor this, lobbying is unlikely to be worthwhile at this stage.

Monitoring the IASB

The IASB sets its standards in public, so it is relatively easy to monitor what is said. You can do this in a number of ways:

The IASB sets its standards in public, so it is relatively easy to monitor what is said

(1) Go to the offices in London and sit in on the meeting that discusses your subject. The agenda is published a few days before the meeting and you have to register to attend.

(2) Listen to a webcast of the meeting, either live or some time in the weeks following the event. Both these methods are effective but time-consuming, and physical presence in London may be expensive, depending on where you are based.

(3) Subscribe to *IFRS Monitor* (www.ifrsmonitor.com), which provides a subscription service that reports on the substantive debate. This is cheaper than attending the meeting and faster than listening to the webcast, as well as providing a written record.

(4) If you subscribe to the IASB's electronic update service, you will receive a summary of the decisions taken at each meeting, but this gives no information about the debate.

(5) Each of the Big Four international audit firms offers some form of IFRS update service, although this may be at too general a level to be useful.

(6) If you want a wider overview of IFRS and the regulatory environment, you can subscribe to *World Accounting Report*, an expensive monthly publication dedicated to the needs of those who are concerned with international financial reporting.

Conclusion

This chapter has looked at how the IASB conducts its standard-setting business, and in particular how it consults widely with constituents as it formulates new standards. The analysis addresses how the individual can interact in the process, and how one can positively lobby the standard-setter. The chapter also includes details of support publications that will help the lobbyist!

CHAPTER 10

HISTORY OF THE IASB

This chapter aims to provide context to the way the IASB works and an understanding of its evolution. The chapter starts chronologically, with the creation of the International Accounting Standards Committee (IASC) and analyses its evolution over what I have called the start-up phase, then consolidation of its position followed by significant change under David Cairns. It then goes on to the IASB and analyses its first decade including its relations with the US and Europe, the convergence process and the financial crisis.

If your main interest in IFRS is their technical content, this chapter will not advance that. However, in my view a knowledge of the history of an organization, particularly one with a difficult political context, is helpful in understanding its decisions. This chapter aims to show where the standard-setter came from and identify something of the political environment within which it works.

With the benefit of hindsight, one can see that the creation of the International Accounting Standards Committee (IASC) in 1973 was very prescient, and yet, like many inventions, it came about almost as an accident. The international standard-setting organization has gone through many metamorphoses since. The nearly 40 years of life of the international standard-setter can be split into four periods: the start-up phase, the development of basic standards, the enhancement phase, and finally the leader of world convergence.

the creation of the IASC ... came about almost as an accident

The start-up phase

The creation and early years of the IASC were dominated by one powerful accountant, Henry Benson. Benson was born in South Africa of British parents. He was in fact the grandson of one of the four Cooper brothers, who started the eponymous audit firm in London in the nineteenth century. The firm operated as Coopers & Lybrand for many years and now survives in the name of PricewaterhouseCoopers. Benson was a driving force in the development of Cooper Bros in the second half of the twentieth century. He was involved in major expansion, including taking the firm into a merger with the US firm Lybrand, Ross Bros and Montgomery in 1957.

Subsequently he became president of his professional body, the Institute of Chartered Accountants in England and Wales (ICAEW). At that time there was no over-arching global organization for accounting professional bodies, but there was an organizing committee that dealt with a world conference that was held every five years. Benson, no longer ICAEW president but a well-known figure in world accounting by then, was asked to chair a committee to look into the future organization of the profession. He presented a report on the committee's work to the 1972 world congress, held in Sydney, Australia.

Listening to this report was Douglas Morpeth, a senior figure in Touche Ross in London and himself president of the ICAEW at that time. Morpeth was also deputy chairman of the newly created UK accounting standard-setter, and he was struck that Benson's report made no mention of an international standard-setter. He telephoned

Benson in his hotel room afterwards and asked why this had not been proposed. Benson was struck by the idea, but was not convinced that the world congress organization was necessarily the best framework.

The two men organized an impromptu meeting with the heads of the Canadian and US delegations to the world congress and agreed the outline of a plan. The IASC would be set up. It was to have nine members, which would be national professional bodies: the US, Canada, Australia, the UK and Ireland, France, Germany, the Netherlands, Mexico and Japan. Benson and Morpeth went back to London and drafted a constitution for this new body. Morpeth organized the support (and funding) of the ICAEW for the project, and in June 1973, the IASC had its first meeting, under the chairmanship of Henry Benson.

Thereafter the IASC was based in London (the IASB remains in London) not least because the ICAEW offered to pay for office space. The American Institute of Certified Public Accountants (AICPA) seconded Paul Rosenfield, one of their senior technical staff, to be the first secretary of the new organization.

In fact the period was one where a great deal of change was taking place in standard-setting. In the US, the Wheat Committee had in 1972 proposed the creation of the Financial Accounting Standards Board to replace the standard-setter provided by the AICPA. In the UK the professional bodies had just created their first standard-setting body. Outside of national standards, the United Nations was also just starting to take an interest with an initiative that led it to issue guidelines on segmental reporting and the Organisation for Economic Cooperation and Development (OECD) began to respond to that.

Steady progress

The IASC proceeded to write International Accounting Standards (IAS). Their first standard, IAS 1, remains in force today, even if much re-organized and revised. The initial standard-setters were not especially trying to break new ground. Benson has written that they were trying to create a set of 'best practice' standards that could be used for international transactions and could also be a benchmark for harmonization. However, best practice did not always mean the same thing to everyone. Where the IASC could not get agreement, in the early days its standards might include more than one option.

The other issue the IASC Board had to face was the lack of take-up of their standards. Each of the member professional associations had to agree to 'use their best endeavours' to have IAS adopted in their country. However, IAS were in fact not used by any of the founding countries until the EU made them compulsory for listed companies in 2005. By the end of the 1970s, there were a number of standards in existence but they were not used. In Europe, some Swiss companies started to use them (there were no Swiss standards for consolidated entities at that time) and the Italian stock exchange regulator also mandated them for use where Italian GAAP had no equivalent.

The standards started to be discussed in teaching texts, as representing some form of benchmark, and they started to be used in former colonies of European countries, particularly those of the UK, as a guide in shaping their own standards. Many professional associations in countries like Singapore or South Africa had used UK practice as their benchmark for developing local standards. As the IASC started to issue standards, these became a more obvious source as being international in nature. However, the IASC came as a result to be seen by some as simply providing standards for developing countries.

They were not the only people trying to work in this area. The UN had set up its Center for Transnational Corporations (CTC) in New York that focused in part on accounting issues, and the OECD had also set up a committee to look at harmonization issues. The IASC was concerned that this would lead to a proliferation of competing international comprehensive bases of accounting. It set out on a diplomatic offensive to persuade these organizations that they should leave standards to the IASC. The IASC were largely successful in convincing these organizations to drop the idea of standard-setting and concentrate on other areas.

The OECD did not develop its accounting further, although it organized meetings between national standard-setters sometimes, and later created a committee for helping former Soviet states to develop accounting rules (based on IAS) and did work in corporate governance. The UN eventually closed the New York CTC but set up a unit in Geneva that continues to provide technical assistance on accounting issues, usually to developing countries, but also holds an annual conference (www.unctad.org/isar). It has produced much material on environmental and social accounting, guidelines for small business and corporate governance. It supports international standards but feels free to work in any area not addressed by the IASB. Its small business accounting guidelines preceded the IASB *IFRS for SMEs*. Some commentators believe that the IASB took up the subject in part because it did not want the UN's guideline becoming the benchmark in that area.

Another significant development during this period was a change in the IASC's relationship with the International Federation of Accountants (IFAC). IFAC had been set up in 1977 at the world congress following the one in which the IASC had first been mooted. Benson had been keen that the IASC should be an entirely independent organization and he and Morpeth had worked hard in the start-up phase to ensure that was the case. However, not everyone shared their view, and once the world profession had established a permanent umbrella organization, there were more calls for the IASC to be housed within that. The IASC was accused of being a rich nations' club where poorer nations could not afford to participate.

The IASC Board members argued that it needed to remain an independent body, and did their best to fight off the IFAC takeover attempt. Of course, precisely the professional organizations that funded the IASC were also leading players in IFAC, and so the different points of view were to be found in individual professional organizations. In the end a compromise was reached, known as the 'mutual commitments'. The IASC would remain independent, but IFAC members

> *the IASC ... established itself as the only international accounting standards-setter*

would automatically become members of the IASC (but not members of its Board). IFAC would fund one developing country to participate in the Board (no costs were reimbursed by IASC, Board members had to fund themselves to attend the meetings held all over the world). IFAC would also nominate members to the Board, while agreeing a standstill for a period.

In later years, there would be other IFAC initiatives to review the relationship between the two bodies, but the 1982 arrangements remained largely in place until 2000 when IFAC agreed to the creation of the IASB as a free-standing non-governmental organization. IFAC developed committees to set audit standards, education standards and public sector accounting standards, but the private sector standards always remained outside its control.

This period can be seen as a consolidation phase, where the IASC issued a significant number of standards, gaining a critical mass in that area, and came to be known more widely around the world. It fought some key battles to be accepted by other international organizations and established itself as the only international accounting standards-setter. Its standards were used as a reference point, without, however, any direct take-up by individual jurisdictions. They were used by some individual companies that wanted to address the international markets as an alternative to US GAAP.

The enhancement phase

Most of the IASC Secretaries had been secondments from other organizations, but in 1985 the IASC appointed a permanent Secretary General, David Cairns. Cairns was a practitioner and academic who had long taken an interest in international accounting, and he set about making a number of reforms. A key issue was that the organization was starved of funds, which were contributed by the member bodies. The structure of the profession in different countries is significantly different. Rich countries such as France, Italy and Germany have restrictive approaches to membership, which meant that the professional associations had relatively few members and little funding available to develop the IASC. However, they were also unwilling to let countries like the US and UK, with much more extensive and therefore wealthier professional organizations, make extra contributions. The IASC's activities were severely constrained by lack of funds.

Cairns noted that the IASC made no money from publishing its standards – the right to publish them was held by the parent national professional associations. He negotiated the right for the IASC itself to publish and sell its work, and released eventually a flow of funding that to this day makes a significant contribution to the organization's funding (the 2009 financial statements show a £5.6m/$8.6m/€6.7m net contribution from publishing).

The new Secretary General also recognized that the IASC style of standard-setting by volunteer representatives of professional associations was disappearing. The anglophone world's first professional standard-setter, the US Financial Accounting Standards Board (FASB), had appeared in 1973, the same year in which the IASC had been formed. It was an augury of the gradual disappearance of standard-setters run by national professional associations in favour of independent professional bodies.

Cairns recognized that increasingly the national associations were no longer significantly involved in standard-setting even though they sat on the IASC Board. He set about encouraging countries like the USA to send FASB members and staff along (Jim Leisenring's long association with international standard-setting derives from this period). He also aimed to persuade the European Commission to get involved. The Commission had from the mid-1960s been trying to harmonize accounting within the EU and had remained largely aloof from the IASC's harmonization efforts. Georges Barthès de Ruyter, president of the IASC 1987–1990, and a prominent figure in French accounting, was a key factor in overcoming this and finally succeeded in persuading the Commission to participate with observer status.

The third fundamental initiative came about, apparently, by chance. As Camfferman and Zeff[1] relate it, David Cairns saw a newspaper article about an upcoming conference of the International Association of Securities Commissions to be held in Paris. Curious to find out more about this other 'IASC' he went along to the conference. This turned out to be the Organisation Internationale de Commissions de Valeurs (OICV), whose official English title is actually the International Organization of Securities Commissions (IOSCO). This was to lead to a relationship that dominated the final decade of the IASC and then to the creation of the IASB.

IOSCO is a global organization for cooperation between national securities regulators. At the time the US Securities and Exchange Commission (SEC) was a major driving force in the development of the organization. An idea they were currently working on was the creation of an international stock exchange passport for secondary listings. A number of leading multinationals were listed on several exchanges in addition to their primary listing (which was usually at their home country exchange). Volvo, for example, was at one time listed on about 18 stock exchanges.

However, secondary listings of this type were generally expensive because most regulators required the foreign company to comply with a modified form of the local listing requirements. IOSCO's idea was that the regulators should get together and specify a uniform package of listing disclosures, which they would then use for companies seeking a secondary listing.

---

1 Camfferman, K. & Zeff, S.A. (2007), *Financial Reporting and Global Capital Markets: A History of the International Accounting Standards Committee, 1973–2000*, Oxford University Press (this is the authorized history of the IASC, an exhaustive and fascinating work compiled by two leading researchers).

The result would be that a single set of financial statements and disclosures could be used all around the world outside a company's home exchange. This would significantly reduce costs and encourage foreign companies to extend their secondary listings. This in turn would bring diversity and choice to investors, who at the time were very reluctant to look outside their domestic markets or were legally constrained from so doing.

Of course, this single passport would have to have financial reporting standards, and with the help of the SEC, the IASC was able to present itself as the essential technical partner to provide the accounting standards. The perfect arrangement from an IASC perspective would have been to be appointed as IOSCO's official standard-setter, with all international accounting standards automatically endorsed. Unfortunately IOSCO was not prepared to go that far: it was happy for the IASC to supply standards, but IOSCO would retain the right to say what standards it wanted and then to review the standards individually.

This was to lead to problems later, but for the immediate, the IASC had found what it had been missing – a client. Up until then the IASC had been busy issuing an increasing number of standards that were influential but not directly adopted by any jurisdiction. At this point people might have been justified in calling it 'just a talking shop' – a comment used much more recently, and unjustifiably, in Europe. Now the IASC had a stock market regulator of sorts for which it would make standards. The relationship gave the IASC a new dignity and provided a clear focus for its work.

IOSCO representatives started to play a role in some IASC committees and the standard-setter started to review its standards. The IASC had to address the fact that many of its standards contained competing options, so two companies could both assert compliance with the standards and yet have significantly different accounting policies. This had to be addressed and the IASC set up the 'Comparability Committee' to look at this. This produced an exposure draft (E32) that set out a series of proposals to reduce the options in the standards. Camfferman and Zeff (op. cit.) say that in discussions the IOSCO representatives had made it clear that if the standards were to be accepted for use in the US, they could not be weaker than US GAAP – an issue that has dominated international standard-setting ever since.

E32 gave way to the Comparability/Improvements project, whose aim was to extend the range of subjects covered by international accounting standards and tighten up the choices available in some of the standards. This was not necessarily an easy process, but it gave point and urgency to the IASC's work.

The IASC had to address the fact that many of its standards contained competing options

The Cairns era, however, was to come to an end in late 1994 after a series of disagreements between the IASC and IOSCO. In 1993 IOSCO had started to talk about a list of core standards that went beyond what the IASC was doing, and of endorsement possibly not arriving for another five years or more. The IASC on the other hand wanted endorsement of those standards that it had improved. IOSCO was unwilling to do that and issued a technical report that accepted a batch of standards while pointing to what it regarded as deficiencies in them.

The IASC leadership were dismayed by this and more than a little angry. They felt that IOSCO representatives had participated closely in the technical programme and, if they had issues, those should have been raised during the improvements process. They also felt that the goalposts had been moved. The chairman at the time, Eiichi Shiratori, addressed the October 1994 IOSCO annual conference in critical terms. David Cairns resigned as Secretary General.

There has been much speculation about why the mood changed at IOSCO. Commentators point to the SEC as being the main opponent of piecemeal endorsement. Some people note that Daimler became the first German company to list in the US in 1993. Up to that point, the conventional thinking had been that development of international accounting standards was a prerequisite to attracting many major European companies to the US markets. It is possible that Daimler's decision persuaded enough people in the US that the tide had turned.

Despite the frustration among the leadership with the perceived change in IOSCO's approach, the secretariat had started to produce a new work plan based on its various exchanges with IOSCO. In May 1995 Bryan Carsberg, a British practitioner turned academic turned regulator, was appointed as the new Secretary General, and with the new Chairman, Michael Sharpe (an Australian who had trained under Henry Benson at Coopers & Lybrand), a new initiative was announced at IOSCO's annual conference in Paris in July 1995. The two organizations held a press conference at which they announced a new work programme to complete a core set of standards by the middle of 1999.

This was the start of what one might now call a 'surge' where the pace of work accelerated and many key standards were written. Bryan Carsberg increased the pressure in 1996 by proposing to move the deadline back to March 1998. He raised fresh funds, took on more staff and increased the number of meetings of the Board to achieve these objectives. A number of key standards were issued during this period, including IAS 34 on interim reporting, IAS 36 on impairment, IAS 37 on provisions, IAS 38 on intangible assets and IAS 39 on financial instruments. In fact the IASC failed to meet the March 1998 deadline, and just managed to agree IAS 39, the most difficult and controversial element of the IOSCO list of core standards, at the very end of 1998.

Transition

The working assumption among the IASC leadership was that IOSCO would indeed this time endorse the standards, and consequently the standard-setter should prepare itself for the next phase of life as the provider of standards to the international capital markets. As early as 1996 the Board agreed to set up a Strategy Working Party to review the functioning of the IASC and make recommendations for its future organization. A discussion paper was issued in December 1998. The future structure of the institution was hotly contested, and remains a matter that some constituents would like to see changed.

Many participants noted that when the IASC Board met, although there were only about 15 members, each delegation consisted of several people, and there were several official observers as well. The result was that usually more than 50 people sat down together to make decisions, and sometimes the numbers rose to perilously near 100. The organization was based on geographical representation with an overlay of interested organizations such as the SEC and European Commission. This contrasts with the US standard-setter, which at the time had seven members.

In effect these are the two competing models that different people favoured: either a geographically representative organization or a small professional committee. If it were a geographically representative body, there was also the question of whether it should represent the countries with the major capital markets, or the countries that used the standards. The structure was hotly debated and alternatives crafted that would square the circle being representational and being a committee of technical experts. The European Union preferred a representative model, while the SEC wanted a structure that resembled the FASB.

The SEC won, and the initial structure of a standard-setting board with 14 members and a group of trustees to oversee the Board and raise money, looks very much the same as the way the FASB was organized at that time, albeit with twice as many Board members. The Trustees were to be appointed on a geographically representative basis – representing capital markets, though, not adopters of the standards. The Board members were to be appointed for their technical competence in reporting to the international financial markets. More representation would be provided through the Standards Advisory Council.

What was much less contested was that the International Federation of Accountants should withdraw completely from the structure, individual national professional associations would no longer contribute or participate, and the new organization would be an independent private sector entity financed by voluntary contributions. At a formal level, the International Federation of Accountants held a conference in Edinburgh in July 2000 and voted through their release of the IASC, paving the way for the IASB.

All that was needed was IOSCO endorsement of the standards. The IASC had duly handed over their finished work at the beginning of 1999, so that this could be sent by IOSCO to its member organizations for evaluation. A year had been allowed for this, with a final decision due in May 2000. The prize that was particularly being sought was that the SEC would agree to accept financial statements based on international standards as equivalent to US GAAP and no longer require foreign companies to reconcile their numbers to US GAAP.

the new organization would be an independent private sector entity financed by voluntary contributions

The prize was not achieved – once again IOSCO did not deliver on the expectations that had been built up. Its May 2000 decision was to approve the core standards, but it did not say its members had to use them as they stood. Its decision was that member regulators could continue to ask for supplementary information to back up the IASC report. Its 1,000-page report also included a detailed list of queries about individual standards.

The IASC was disappointed but it had at least achieved IOSCO endorsement of the core standards. Some people would also have argued that SEC recognition was always unlikely at that point, given that the US regulator had made clear it wanted to assess not only the standards but also the application of those standards by companies, the level of compliance and the quality of the audit.

Very few companies in the world actually used international standards at that time, and many of those who did so did not necessarily comply with all the standards. This was very much the case in France in the 1990s where the abuse of international standards was such that company law was changed and the stock exchange regulator forbade any reference to the standards. Nonetheless it was a growing practice, particularly in continental Europe, for the largest multinational companies to provide consolidated accounts using either US GAAP or international standards.

Although the European Commission had started a regional harmonization programme in 1966, it made an announcement in 1995 that it was not planning to harmonize further, and that individual states should look to the IASC if they wanted to develop their reporting for groups. The harmonization programme had achieved a certain amount of uniformity where previously there had been quite divergent approaches, but the Commission had been unable to persuade member states to fund any kind of ongoing standard-setting programme. There was indeed scepticism as to what purpose regional standards could serve, given that there were already two models used internationally, US GAAP and IASC standards. As noted, a number of states had progressively allowed companies active in more than one capital market to use US GAAP or IASC standards.

The Commission had nonetheless remained cool towards the IASC and it was something of a shock to the accounting world when it announced in June 2000 that it would require European listed companies to use IASC standards from 2005. With the benefit of hindsight, one can see that the Commission's timing was wrong. If it had wanted to have a bigger hand in shaping the future IASB, it should have declared its intent two years earlier. Alternatively, it should have waited another year at least and started independent negotiations when it could have argued for changes in the structure in return for the massive boost of credibility it provided to the international standard-setter.

As it was, the Commission announcement meant that IFAC and the IASC went into their July 2000 meeting much cheered, instead of being a little gloomy about IOSCO's less than full endorsement of the standards. However, the Commission had no special place in the structure and indeed was deemed to have accepted the structure as developed with an eye on IOSCO and the SEC. Nonetheless it had in effect supplanted IOSCO and become the new main client of the IASC.

Global convergence

The first public meeting of the International Accounting Standards Board (IASB) took place at a hotel in London in April 2001. Part of its arrangements were that, like the FASB, it would set standards 'in the sunshine' – meetings of the Board would be held in public when dealing with standards (but not administrative matters). The public gallery was very full as many of the 'great and the good' of international accounting came along to see the start of this major development. Just like the original IASC the Board was situated in London (there had been a brief flirtation with the idea of being based in Lille, in northern France, but this failed to gain traction). Just like the original IASC, the Board had a British head.

The new Board was chaired by David Tweedie, previously a partner in KPMG and then chairman for 10 years of the UK standard-setter. Of the original 14 members, only four did not have English as their mother tongue. Two of the Board members were former members of the FASB (Jim Leisenring and Tony Cope) while three others (Mary Barth, Tom Jones and Bob Herz) had been closely involved with US standard-setting. Tricia O'Malley was a former chairman of the Canadian standard-setter. Bob Herz subsequently left the IASB to become chairman of the FASB. The North American input was considerable. In addition, many of the members had also participated in the G4+1 group of standard-setters, an informal working group for anglophone national standard-setters (there is more discussion of Board composition in Chapter 11).

The first meetings were much concerned about fixing the agenda of the standard-setter. A priority was to amend the rules on business combinations and those on intangible assets to reflect the significant changes the FASB had introduced. The FASB had abandoned merger accounting but no longer required goodwill to be amortized. The IASB needed to follow suit, and this concern eventually gave rise to IFRS 3 and amendments to IAS 38. It was also clear that the existing requirements for first time adoption were not sufficiently detailed and were difficult to apply. The IASB started work on what became IFRS 1.

Finally the IASB took up the problematic issue of stock options. The FASB had been unable to make US corporations apply fully a standard that required employee stock options to be treated as an expense. Some European countries where the practice of issuing such compensation was growing also wanted guidance. The IASB decided that this would be a 'leadership project' – a topic where the international standard-setter had a unique advantage. Some members of the Standards Advisory Council gave dire warnings and noted that US corporations had spent $80m lobbying against the FASB standard.

Nonetheless the IASB went ahead and IFRS 2 was the result – and the world did not come to an end. However, the IASB had accidentally benefited from chaos in the US. The Enron scandal, and the others that came to light as recession took a hold, had dented American confidence in the effectiveness of its financial reporting. By comparison, the international approach looked more attractive. The Sarbanes Oxley Act, the US response to Enron, mandated the SEC to carry out a study of principles-based standards. This study called for the abandonment of FASB standards with 'bright lines' and the development of objectives-based standards, more like those of the IASB.

At those first meetings, one of the things that was remarkable was that much of the focus was on the US. My notes show that in discussing agenda items, there was hardly any mention of the IOSCO criticisms of the standards, and no discussion of the need to ensure that the standards were fit for adoption in Europe in 2004/5. The Board did discuss a programme of improvements to the existing standards, but the debate was couched in terms of repairing faults so that the standards were of an acceptable quality, not about getting ready for Europe. Although as time went by concern about being ready for 2004/5 became much more apparent, there is some justification for the view that the IASB at that time was heavily oriented towards convergence with the US, and paid little attention to Europe.

Relations with the US

Initially the IASB arranged to have one joint meeting a year with the FASB, but in September 2002 it signed the 'Norwalk Agreement' with the FASB. This set out a programme of convergence which involved both work on joint projects and removal of differences where feasible.

Not least, out of this agreement came a decision to update their respective conceptual frameworks and to converge on a common framework. The number of joint meetings was increased to two a year, one in London and the other in Norwalk, Connecticut. Ever since then, the two Boards have worked closely together.

This cooperation was extended by a 2006 Memorandum of Understanding. The European Commission had been talking with the SEC about removing the reconciliation that the SEC required from foreign issuers listed in the US. The Commission was talking about introducing such a requirement in Europe for any company not using IFRS. The two institutions agreed a road map for doing away with the reconciliation requirement and recognizing IFRS and US GAAP as equivalent (the holy grail long sought by the IASC). The SEC then sat down with the FASB and IASB to discuss what progress towards convergence it wanted

in September 2002 [the IASB] signed the 'Norwalk Agreement' with the FASB

to see in place before it would do this. The Memorandum of Understanding set out a series of milestones to be achieved by 2008.

The standard-setters duly worked on this, albeit not as successfully in terms of the speed of decision-making as they had imagined. However, well before the 2008 deadline the SEC suddenly announced that it was satisfied, and that financial reports drawn up under IFRS would be considered as equivalent to US GAAP and no reconciliation was necessary after 2007. The prize envisaged when David Cairns first talked to the SEC in 1987 had finally been gained 20 years later.

However, the SEC did not stop there; in 2008 it issued a road map for the adoption of IFRS in the US in place of US standards. It proposed that a decision be made in 2011 and asked for feedback. The SEC, FASB and IASB then sat down again and prepared a revised Memorandum of Understanding, with milestones to be achieved by June 2011 (also the date at which David Tweedie steps down as chairman of the IASB).

Of course there was then a change of US government and a new chairman of the SEC. Nothing was heard of the feedback on the SEC's proposed road map for many months. But in February 2010 the SEC declared itself. Adoption was still possible but not as early as the 2008 road map suggested. A decision would be taken at the end of 2011, and if this was for adoption, it would not occur before 2015 or 2016. In the meantime the SEC staff would evaluate issues of compliance, interpretation and comparability in reports produced under IFRS, and assess the IASB's independence.

Relations with Europe

If things were going relatively well in relations with the US, the reverse was the case with Europe. Many people in Europe had been totally ignorant of the existence of international accounting standards before the European Union's decision to adopt them, formalized in a 2002 Regulation. So while the people managing the IASB felt that they were part of a long-running process in which the individuals had been involved for years, their new 'clients' thought that the standards had only become significant with EU adoption. There was a mismatch of perceptions that led Europe to feel ignored by the IASB and the IASB to feel Europe was trying to take them over.

On top of that, the European Commission had set up machinery for endorsement of IFRS that gave endless opportunities for politics and revisiting old decisions. The EU Regulation requiring use of IFRS overrides national legislation, but it requires that each and every standard receives formal approval by the EU (it created its Accounting Regulatory Committee, consisting of representatives of member states) so that it becomes part of EU law in itself. The Commission approved the creation of a private sector advisory body, the European Financial Reporting Advisory Group (EFRAG). This body does detailed work on standards and liaises with the IASB and subsequently advises the Commission on the suitability of an IFRS for endorsement. The IFRS is submitted for approval to the Accounting Regulatory Committee (ARC), but its decisions are subject to the oversight of the European Parliament and the European Council of Ministers.

The first problem arose from the endorsement of IAS 39 on financial instruments. French banks did not like many aspects of this, but in particular they did not like what is called the 'demand deposit floor'. The standard says a liability cannot be recorded at less than is susceptible to be repaid on demand. This means that retail banks account for client current accounts at their book value. However, national practice is to discount these, on the basis that, although the money in the account churns, there is a predictable permanent balance on a portfolio of accounts, which constitutes a medium- to long-term loan.

The IASB refused to change this and the ARC refused to endorse this part of the standard. The ARC cannot add anything, it can only delete, which is what it did: a clause was 'carved out' of the standard.

The carve-out, though small, has caused endless problems. EU listed companies are supposed to say in their accounting principles note that they follow 'IFRS as approved for use in the EU' and the auditors have to attest this. For all but a handful of companies this has absolutely no effect on their numbers and they comply with IFRS as issued by the IASB. However, if they wish to assert that, this has to be a separate assertion and the auditor has also to attest to that as well. The reason this is important is that the right not to produce a reconciliation for the SEC is restricted to companies that assert compliance with IFRS as issued by the IASB.

Europe has also run a campaign right from the early days along the lines that the governance structure of the IASB and the Foundation does not provide enough public accountability. Europeans often say also that the US is too heavily represented in the organization while people who actually use the standards are under-represented. The Commission has ground away at the Trustees, and the European Parliament has called for greater European input to the standard-setter.

Over time they have succeeded in having changes made. The first move was for the Trustees to increase the number of Trustees in the foundation, giving Europe equal representation with the USA. The first chairman of the Trustees was Paul Volker, the former chairman of the US Federal Reserve. However, since he stepped down, the chairman has been a European.

In 2008 the Trustees agreed to some significant constitutional changes. They agreed that the IASB itself should become subject to geographical constraints, with the membership eventually increased to 16 from 2012. They also set up the Monitoring Board, which started work in 2009. This is supposed to represent the world's capital markets, and has oversight of the Trustees' decision-making, including appointments of future trustees and standard-setters. The members of the Monitoring Board are representatives of the SEC, the Financial Services Agency of Japan, the European Commission and two people from IOSCO.

The financial crisis

The most significant event for the IASB in this turbulent first decade has to be the financial crisis. All sorts of politicians and others who until then had thought accounting was not worth spending any money on, suddenly got the idea that it was crucial in maintaining world financial stability. This sudden interest caught the IASB and FASB unawares but eventually triggered a massive re-think of their financial instrument accounting. It also triggered interest in convergence from the governments of the world's 20 largest countries (G20).

The banking crisis was blamed by some bankers on the requirement under US GAAP and IFRS to report many financial assets at fair value. As the sub-prime loan panic grew, the financial markets seized up because people were suspicious of the value of assets and preferred to stay liquid. This meant that market values plummeted and banks that were required to mark to market ended up recording losses.

The most significant event for the IASB in this turbulent first decade has to be the financial crisis

The argument then went in different directions. Politicians and others started saying that marking to market had created paper profits for banks in the economic upswing and encouraged them to over-extend and now they were being obliged to sell in fire sale markets. They said fair value accounting was 'pro-cyclical' – it exaggerated the economic cycle – and it should be abandoned.

Standard-setters responded by saying that if the market was illiquid, fair value could not be determined from the market and must be calculated on the underlying cash flows. Banks were not reading the rules correctly. They also pointed out that financial reporting is there to give transparent information, what investors do with the information is their concern.

The problems caused a crisis in relations with the European Commission. They told the IASB in October 2008 that either the IASB relaxed a rule forbidding reclassification of financial assets, or the Commission would make another carve-out from IAS 39 to remove that rule. The IASB reacted urgently on the grounds that a further carve-out would precipitate a crisis of confidence in its standards. However, the IASB's reaction in turn sparked concerns in the US and elsewhere about political interference and the independence of the standard-setter.

On the wider political stage, the G20 group of world leaders started to meet regularly to handle the financial crisis. It charged the Financial Stability Board (FSB), an offshoot of the international bank regulatory organization in Basel, with reviewing standards governing bank behaviour. This remit was much wider than accounting, but did include accounting nonetheless. The standard-setters were told to simplify their financial instrument accounting. At its Pittsburgh Summit in 2009 the G20 formally charged the IASB and FASB with converging their standards by June 2011, and told the IASB to improve its governance structure. The standard-setters set up financial crisis teams and launched a programme of monthly joint meetings, either taking place physically or via a videolink between Norwalk and London.

While the IASB and FASB were encouraged to converge as quickly as possible, they were also subject to different pressures to simplify and renew rapidly their financial instrument accounting. There was certainly no time to create a new joint project and re-think financial instrument accounting from a zero base. The consequence was agreement on reducing the classifications of financial assets to two, but the FASB seems set to measure both at fair value. The FSB had told the two boards that it did not want to see any increased use of fair value. The IASB listened and one category of financial assets is at amortized cost with the other at fair value.

The two standard-setters have accelerated their work programmes and put everyone linked with them under great pressure in a manner reminiscent of the 1996–98 rush to complete the IOSCO core standards. It seems unlikely that they will achieve their MoU objectives within 2011, but it is not clear how strongly the G20 will react, given that the initial pressure of the financial crisis is in the past.

Conclusion

This chapter has been a brief tour of the highlights of the creation of the IASC and its evolution into the IASB. The IASC seemed like a good thing to be doing but no one knew what to do with its standards. It was not until the crucial 1987–93 phase that the organization acquired focus and a specific purpose. Circumstances since then, particularly adoption by the EU and probably the Enron and other US scandals, have conspired to confirm and expand the role of the international standard-setter. It has, so far, survived the financial crisis, and gained a great deal more governmental visibility.

There are, of course, challenges ahead. Major economies such as Canada, Brazil, India and South Korea are adopting IFRS while Japan and China are 'converging' their standards. This will put pressure on the issues of uniform application and compliance. If the IASB survives those, there is then the challenge of the US adopting IFRS. Some commentators think that US adoption should be avoided since the very particular and very litigious cultural environment would push IFRS into a confined set of anti-abuse rules unsuitable for an international and multicultural environment.

CHAPTER 11

OBSERVER NOTES

This chapter discusses the composition and behaviour of the IASB from the perspective of one who has spent 10 years observing the public standard-setting process. The chapter looks at the changes in composition of the Board over the first decade. It notes that decisions are a majority position and that the IASB can have no opinions as such. However, it then goes on to discuss underlying themes that can be discerned in Board decisions, including the use of the Conceptual Framework, fair value, executory contracts and anti-abuse measures. It also considers the Board use of the 'true and fair view'.

This final chapter is a set of reflections on the standard-setting process in general, and on the IASB in particular. I have spent many, many hours in the boardroom at 30 Cannon Street and elsewhere, listening to the members of the IASB (sometimes joined by the FASB) debating accounting issues during its first decade. In the coffee breaks, the hard core of about four or five observers who attend most meetings often discuss the object of their study. This chapter is the sort of thing we talk about.

Standard-setters are people

The first issue is that the IASB is a collection of people, originally 14, now 15 and in 2012, 16. They each have opinions, sometimes strongly held, sometimes less so. Commentators tend to say: 'The IASB thinks this …' or 'The IASB does this …', which implies that the IASB is a single, coherent institution with a single point of view. Of course that is not the case, and when the IASB takes an official line, this is the result of a debate and a majority vote.

During the standard-setting process, the same issues will be debated several times, and the less there is agreement, the more often a subject will be debated. There is generally a spectrum of opinion within the Board, with some at each extreme and some in the middle – 'floating voters'. As a consequence you can have (say) a vote 8–7, which is insufficient to pass an exposure draft (a super majority of nine is needed). There is a further debate and one or two people who are in the middle will think to themselves that they will maybe change their vote so that a decision can be taken. Also people have different states of mind on different days. Someone who has stepped off a transatlantic flight straight into the boardroom will have a different frame of mind from someone who has slept in their own bed and just made a short commute within London. In a close vote, two people changing their mind can switch the Board between two completely opposite points of view.

the IASB is a collection of people

It should be said that this is even more marked with the FASB where voting is by simple majority, not super majority. In a 2–2 vote with the fifth member undecided, in effect the fifth member makes the decision – but they might feel differently about it the next day. As a consequence, it is impossible for the IASB or FASB to have a totally coherent line in standard-setting, and their decisions taken together can seem inconsistent. Equally, during the process of debate from discussion paper to exposure draft to final standard each issue is re-debated over a long period, which is also conducive to changes of mind. A case in point was in 2009 when the IASB voted that using full fair value for financial instruments was neither realistic nor desirable. They year before they had issued a document suggesting that full fair value was the preferred route.

This need for a majority vote is also affected by the systematic replacement of Board members. The initial term of office is five years, but previous appointments have been staggered so that some Board members stand down every year – three a year in a steady state, but there never is a steady state. Members can serve two terms, but the second is now limited to three years. The effect of this is that every year there are some new members of the Board. Bearing in mind that even a simple standard takes three years and five years is a more realistic rule of thumb, this means that the composition of the Board will change more or less significantly during the progress of a project. In a close vote, this too can impact where is the majority on a particular issue.

One of the implications of this is that as the composition of the Board changes, so the consensus between the majority also changes, and this will have an effect on the standards produced. It is obvious that IAS 1, first issued in 1976, and still in force, even if much changed over the years, is likely to be different from IFRS 9 issued in 2009. IAS 1 was written by a volunteer group of the 'great and the good' from the professional bodies of the developed nations. IFRS 9 was written by a 15-person professional Board under pressure from the G20 governments.

What sort of people?
The IASB Constitution specifies that Board members must represent the 'best available combination of technical expertise and diversity of international business and market experience' (Paragraph 25). The Constitution adds: 'The Trustees shall select IASB members so that the IASB as a group provides an appropriate mix of recent practical experience among auditors, preparers, users and academics'.

A number of commentators have attempted to analyse the Board members in terms of their professional background, but this is not that simple an exercise. On the one hand, in many anglophone countries, a training as a public accountant is regarded as the appropriate route for anyone interested in a career in accounting in any context. This means that most anglophone standard-setters have started their career in an audit firm, but it does not mean that it is reasonable to categorize them as auditors.

Simplifications about the approach of the individual standard-setter are to be avoided

To take an example, Tom Jones, in 2001 the first deputy chairman of the IASB, and now retired, is a British chartered accountant, trained with an international firm. But like many public accountants, he decided before he had been 10 years in the business to switch to working for a preparer. He worked in a number of different European countries for different companies until he started to work for Citibank. Eventually he was transferred to New York and became vice-president (accounting) for Citibank. He lives in Connecticut, USA, just down the road from the FASB, on whose committees he served in the 1990s. Although he is an expert on accounting by banks, and trained as an auditor, you cannot pigeonhole him as a bank accountant or an auditor, nor even really as bringing British experience, given that much of his career has been spent in other countries.

Simplifications about the approach of the individual standard-setter are to be avoided. Tom Jones is far from exceptional in terms of crossing a number of cultural boundaries. That said, I think it is possible to observe a change in the type of person that the Trustees have picked as Board members over time. Table 7 shows the composition of the founding Board in April 2001.

What Table 7 tells us is that the original Board had people who had mostly a wide background experience, but the majority (10 of 14) were native English speakers. Eight have been classified as auditors,

Table 7 Professional experience of 2001 IASB

Board member	Standard-setter	Auditor	Preparer	Academic	User	Anglophone upbringing	Non-anglo-phone
Mary Barth		✓		✓		✓	
Hans-Georg Bruns			✓				✓
Tony Cope	✓				✓	✓	
Bob Garnett		✓	✓		✓	✓	
Gilbert Gélard		✓	✓				✓
Tom Jones			✓			✓	
Jim Leisenring	✓	✓				✓	
Warren McGregor	✓					✓	
Tricia O'Malley	✓	✓				✓	
Harry Schmid			✓				✓
Bob Herz		✓				✓	
David Tweedie	✓	✓				✓	
Geoff Whittington	✓			✓		✓	
Tatsumi Yamada		✓					✓

although another three received their initial accounting training in the audit industry.

We can contrast this with the Board as at 1 January 2011, as shown in Table 8. This information is drawn largely from the IASB website, and to the extent that the website gives partial information, this may be incomplete. I have not been able to establish whether Warren McGregor and Darrell Scott started out their careers in public accounting firms, as one would predict given their background.

The change in composition of the IASB can be summarized as shown in Table 9.

One should be wary of drawing too much from this information, given that some people have wider experience than others. For example, Bob Garnett has experience as an auditor, a preparer and a user, although in debate he mostly spoke from the viewpoint of a preparer, in my opinion. However, the fact that he had user experience means that

Table 8 Professional experience of IASB January 2011

Board member	Standard-setter	Auditor	Preparer	Academic	User	Regulator	Anglo-phone	Non-anglo-phone
Steve Cooper		✓			✓		✓	
Philippe Danjou		✓				✓		✓
Jan Engstrom			✓					✓
Pat Finnegan		✓			✓		✓	
Amaro Gomes						✓		✓
P Kalavacherla		✓						✓
Elke Koenig			✓					✓
Pat McConnell					✓		✓	
Warren McGregor	✓						✓	
Paul Pacter	✓	✓					✓	
Darrell Scott			✓				✓	
John Smith		✓					✓	
David Tweedie	✓	✓					✓	
Tatsumi Yamada		✓						✓
Zhang Wei-Guo	✓			✓		✓		✓

Table 9 Summary of standard-setters' backgrounds

Experience	2001	2011
Standard-setter	6	4
Auditor	8	8
Preparer	5	3
User	2	3
Regulator	0	3
Academic	2	1
Anglophone	10	8
Non-anglophone	4	7

the original IASB is analysed here as including two users, whereas only Tony Cope visibly maintained links with the analyst community.

I would draw two conclusions from the changes: (1) that the original IASB included a lot of people who had worked as standard-setters; and (2) if you consider regulators to be surrogates for users, the Board is now dominated by users. There has also been a move away from the absolute domination of the Board by members with English as their mother tongue.

The first point is not very surprising, given that many of the Board members had worked together in the G4+1 group of anglophone standard-setters. At the time the argument was that if you wanted a full-time international standard-setting Board, you needed people with national standard-setting experience. However, if you start from that assumption, you end up with Anglo-Saxons, because this kind of private sector standard-setting is typical of the anglophone world.

Moving on from there, if the object of the Board is to set standards that provide information that is useful to users, there is an argument to include users as standard-setters. The counter-argument there is that the people with standard-setting experience are supposed to come to a judgement that balances user usefulness against preparer and auditor cost. However, regulators presumably also have some of the same exposure and experience.

What do they think?

I have made the point that there is no such thing as a group ideology within the IASB, and that the standards emanating from the Board can move through 180° depending upon where the voters in the middle ground settle. You cannot therefore deduce a coherent group position by looking at outputs. With that very important caveat, I am going to offer a little subjective analysis of some underlying notions that have more or less been upheld during the first decade of the IASB's activity.

It is a central part of the FASB's mandate that the Board should write standards that are consistent with its Conceptual Framework. There are strong historical reasons for this. The FASB was created as a result of a crisis in US standard-setting where the standard-setter, run by the American Institute of Certified Public Accountants (AICPA), was perceived to be in the hands of the large audit firms. It was thought to issue standards that met the needs of interest groups and did not give consistent accounting.

Leaving aside the question of whether those views were justified, in the early 1970s the AICPA set up two committees: the Wheat Committee, to look at what kind of structure an independent standard-setter should have; and the Trueblood Committee, to look at what framework would give consistent standards. The outcome was the FASB and its Conceptual Framework.

there is no such thing as a group ideology within the IASB

The IASB's predecessor (the IASC) eventually created a Conceptual Framework, as discussed in the appendix to Chapter 2, derived from the US original. The IASB's constitution requires Board members to set standards consistent with that framework. So the first principle is that new standards should be coherent with the Conceptual Framework. If they are not, that does not make them invalid, however, but the IASB has to justify its position. In fact the IASB makes frequent and overt use of the Conceptual Framework in constructing new standards. That is a fundamental principle – perhaps **the** fundamental principle.

The Framework says that the objective of financial reporting is to provide information that is useful to providers of capital in making investment decisions. So the second fundamental principle of the IASB is that its standards are directed essentially at the capital markets and investors and must be decision-useful. A corollary of this is that a change in standards must result in **better** information, and the costs of providing it must be outweighed by the benefits. This is a point frequently used by commentators who ask that the IASB point out why a change gives better information.

Focusing on decision-useful information for capital markets is something the IFRS Foundation views as uncontroversial, as does the SEC and the International Organization of Securities Commissions (IOSCO). I would say that for much of the first decade of the IASB, members applied this approach unquestioningly. However, by the end of the decade this was beginning to change. The G20 heads of governments and the EU do not now agree with the capital market approach. Although the EU signed up in 2002 to avowedly market-oriented standards, it now feels, as a result of the financial crisis, that the standard-setter should also favour the stability of the financial markets.

The G20 mandated the Financial Stability Board (consisting largely of bank and market regulators and housed at the Bank for International Settlements in Basel) to work with the IASB and FASB to achieve convergence by June 2011. In an October 2010 speech in the US, EU Commissioner Barnier argued for US adoption of IFRS, saying that there was no point in worldwide prudential ratios in banking if people did not use the same accounting standards to draw up financial statements. Clearly he thinks that IFRS should be useful for regulating banks.

The other fundamental implication of the Conceptual Framework as applied by the IASB in the last decade is that accounting is triggered by a change in assets or liabilities. This is a controversial issue but far from being a new one. Historians would argue that in the nineteenth century, financial reporting was balance sheet oriented (no income statement was even provided), and it was only in the twentieth century that attention shifted to measuring income. The reasons for this are many, but people point to the progressive introduction of income tax, necessitating a measure of income, and anti-abuse arguments about the availability of profit for dividends.

The accounting world is divided between those who see measuring profit on transactions as the driving force in financial statements, with the balance sheet numbers as a residual of the income measurement process, and those who see measuring assets and liabilities as the key, with changes in net assets being the profit or loss for the year. This does make some difference. The asset and liability approach, particularly grounded in the Conceptual Framework definition of an asset (embodies a future benefit, controlled by the company and arising from a past event), would mean that expenses and revenues are less frequently deferred to future periods because they do not represent a future benefit, they are merely smoothing costs or revenues.

An example of this would be negative goodwill under IFRS 3 *Business Combinations*. If the fair value of the acquired assets and liabilities is greater than the consideration, negative goodwill arises. The standard requires this to be taken to profit and loss at once. A transaction-oriented person might argue that the negative goodwill arises because the purchaser expects some initial losses, and the credit should be released to income over the period when those losses are expected to occur.

A balance sheet-oriented standard-setter looking to write some rules to address a particular situation will look at changes in assets and liabilities created. The standard-setter looking to measure income will look at whether revenue is generated or not. If the measurement basis is historical cost the difference between the two is, though, relatively minor in practice and largely comes down to the timing of expenses and revenues. The transaction approach believes in what Jim Leisenring, the doyen of Anglo-Saxon standard-setters, always describes as 'smoooooothing' revenue and expenses. Expenditure is held in the balance sheet until revenue arrives to trigger expensing of the matching costs.

The asset and liability people prefer not to defer. Where the different approaches will provide significantly different measurement is if the measurement basis is some form of current value, such as fair value. The asset and liability approach will generate fair value gains and losses attributable to movements in the market, while these will not be recognized under an income approach.

The majority view of the IASB during the first decade of this century has been that any recognition decision starts with a discussion of whether any assets or liabilities have been created or changed. They interpret the framework firmly as requiring that the preparer report to investors on changes in the assets and liabilities from the beginning to the end of the reporting period, eventually analysing these between operating income and Other Comprehensive Income. IASB member Philippe Danjou says that it seems easier from a standard-setting point of view to define the attributes of an asset and a liability than the attributes of revenue or expense. Contracts generally create rights and obligations which turn into revenues and expenses.

Fair value controversies

This approach has led some people to accuse the Board of working systematically towards a full fair value world where all assets and liabilities were stated at fair value. While it is true that one or two Board members are fully paid up members of the fair value party, no Board member thinks it remotely likely that a full fair value balance sheet could be mandated in the foreseeable future. It should also be borne in mind that the timescale of standard-setting, and the extent of the literature (full IFRS when published in hard copy runs to more than 2,000 pages), mean that even if a particular set of Board members had a strong ideology, they would not be able to move the corpus of IFRS other than fairly marginally during their term on the Board.

Notwithstanding that, if there is one issue that has dominated the first decade of the IASB, it is the use of fair value as a measurement basis. This is, of course, much overstated. The fact of the matter is that at least back to the nineteenth century fair value has been used in financial reporting to provide financial values to transactions that are not denominated in money terms. This happens frequently, for example, when an unincorporated business decides to incorporate. The owners 'sell' the existing assets and liabilities to the new company in exchange for shares. Usually the value of the transaction is done at fair value to provide a 'deemed cost'. Using a measurement basis other than historical cost is also regarded as uncontroversial in inflationary economies.

Where the IASB (and FASB) have hit trouble is the use of current value for financial assets and liabilities. The use of sophisticated financial instruments only started in the 1980s and there were no accounting rules (most national jurisdictions still have none). Historical cost is misleading because often there is no cost, for example to enter a forward contract, or the cost may be relatively small in relation to the underlying values, such as for an option. However, the economic implications may be significant and are not reflected in the balance sheet under a historical cost system. The standard-setter response was to measure using fair value on a continuing basis. This reflects the underlying economics of the executory contracts at a given point in time.

However, using fair value leads into a host of application problems: are all financial assets and liabilities measured this way? Are changes in fair value recognized in the income statement or in equity? When a financial instrument is used for hedging, does this alter the way in which fair value changes are recognized? How do you calculate fair value when there is no active market? These questions occupied the IASB and FASB in the 1990s and resurfaced in the financial crisis, and are probably the source of perceived constituent discontent about the use of fair value. Now people accept that some instruments should be at fair value but disagree where the line is drawn. They also disagree as to whether fair value changes should go through the income statement. The EU, for example, now complains (as the French have been doing for many years) that the use of fair value imports volatility into the balance sheet, and financial stability requires that this should not happen.

using fair value leads into a host of application problems

I think that the original IASB had a goodly number of people who thought fair value was the answer to quite a lot of problems. I should point out that the developed world experienced a bout of severe inflation in the 1970s, with annual inflation going to more than 20% in countries such as France and the UK. The FASB mandated inflation accounting disclosures, and the UK standard-setter tried unsuccessfully to replace historical cost with 'current cost' accounting. Most of today's preparers and auditors are too young to have experienced that, but many of the IASB's founder members lived through it or had their training in a period when the key financial reporting issue was inflation. Geoff Whittington (IASB member 2001–2006), for example, is a leading author on the subject. That experience leaves you with a heightened scepticism about the value of historical cost numbers, and that is a factor that should be remembered when considering people's enthusiasm for alternative measurement approaches.

Executory contracts

One area where standard-setters with an asset and liability approach may differ significantly from transaction-oriented standard-setters is that of executory contracts. This is a problem that is not much discussed in policy circles. An executory contract is a contract that has been signed but not yet executed. Such a contract, for example an agreement to buy a car that will be delivered in three months' time, will appear in the income statement when the transaction is performed and the goods or services are passed to the client. A forward contract to buy currency is another form of executory contract.

Such contracts are not significant in all sectors: a retailer has few such contracts with customers but may have more with suppliers. However, the value of executory contracts could be an important piece of information for investors about future cash flows. Traditionally the only executory contract that is acknowledged in financial reporting is what IAS 37 *Provisions, contingent liabilities and contingent assets* would refer to as an 'onerous contract'. Conventional prudence requires that a foreseeable loss is recognized when it can be predicted, and so where an executory contract is perceived to be loss-making, the full expected loss should be provided for at once. Transaction-based standard-setters would say that you recognize nothing until the transaction is complete, except for reflecting a prudence override.

Where IASB members have an asset and liability orientation, and this is combined with a feeling that they should recognize open positions that impact economic value, there is more enthusiasm for recognizing executory contracts. The argument would be that where a company has executory contracts, these represent future cash flows that impact the current value of the company. This can be seen, of course, in the use of fair value for some financial instruments. Remeasuring to fair value at balance sheet date enables you to simulate completion of the executory contract by telling you what you would have to pay or what you would receive if you closed out the contract at balance sheet date.

I would argue that recognition of executory contracts, and even obligations where there is no contract, has been part of the predominant approach of the IASB in the first decade. This can be seen in the revenue recognition project, where the entity recognizes an executory contract as a performance obligation and a financial asset as soon as the contract exists. Similarly the leasing project proposes that lessees recognize a lease obligation and corresponding right of use asset for the **expected** period of the lease, potentially going well beyond the period of the contract.

Of course the boundary of what is recognized and measured in financial reporting is an artificial one, determined under IFRS by what standard-setters think meets the asset and liability definitions of the framework and what the preparer and auditor think can be measured with sufficient reliability. Everyone would agree that there are assets and liabilities that do not get recognized because they fail one or other of these tests even if they may well have economic value. What appears to have happened during the first decade is that this boundary has moved to take in more unrealized transactions. However, whether this will continue into the next decade is debatable, given the gradual retirement of what I could call the 'inflation generation'.

True and fair view

European accounting directives, which IFRS may not contravene if they are to be used in the EU, require that the financial statements give a 'true and fair view' of the financial situation of the company. There is an extensive literature on what this may mean, and one view is that it is an overriding quality that the financial statements should not be misleading. Despite the prominence of this concept in European law and in debate about accounting, especially in the UK where the notion originated, it does **not** appear to be part of the IASB's collective thinking.

IAS 1 *Presentation of Financial Statements* says that compliance with IFRS will normally 'fairly represent' (= give a true and fair view) of the financial situation, as discussed earlier in Chapter 2. Sir David Tweedie, first chairman of the IASB and former chairman of the UK Accounting Standards Board, fought very hard in the early part of the first decade to retain the concept when American members of the IASB were trying to remove it; Board members hardly ever mention it in debate. Essentially in their thinking, the Conceptual Framework could be taken as a detailed elaboration of what is meant by the true and fair view, and so it is sufficient to comply with the framework.

Anti-abuse measures

However, one qualitative characteristic that is **not** in the framework, but which is very much observed in writing standards, is that standards should mitigate abuse by preparers and eventually auditors. Inevitably those IASB members who are most strongly concerned about abuse are US auditors and users. The US environment is one where preparers have the reputation of pushing the rules to their literal limits in order to get the most favourable presentation of their entity's financial position. This, and the attendant fear of very expensive litigation if people go too far, is usually given as the reason why the FASB prefers rules-based standards with 'bright lines' to make it clear what is allowed and what is not.

One place where an anti-abuse approach can be seen is in the IASB's rules for hedge accounting. IAS 39 *Financial Instruments: Recognition and Measurement* requires that derivatives are measured at fair value through profit and loss. However, the idea of hedging is that you enter into a contract, maybe a derivative, which has an equal and opposite risk to the contract you want to protect. When this latter contract matures, you want to recognize the gain or loss on the hedging instrument at the same time, so that they cancel each other out. This means that recognition of gains and losses on a derivative can be deferred if it is a hedging instrument but must be recognized immediately if not.

One place where an anti-abuse approach can be seen is in the IASB's rules for hedge accounting

From an abuse perspective, that puts pressure on what is allowed to be accounted for as a hedge, because in effect management can choose when to recognize gains and losses on a derivative depending on how they designate it. Consequently the rules for allowing hedge designation are complex and in practice limit the number of hedges recognized. A hedging instrument must be designated as such as soon as it is acquired, the designation must be documented, cannot be changed and it must be 'effective'. If the hedge responds differently to the market than the contract that is being hedged by more than 20%, the hedge is deemed ineffective and must be abandoned. In the revision of IAS 39 the IASB are trying to make the hedge accounting requirements simpler and more responsive to the way financial institutions in particular manage risk. However, every debate as the new approach is explored is virtually a dialogue between the staff and a former New York auditor who thinks they are leaving open too many abuse opportunities.

Generally when the IASB debates almost any issue, someone or other will ask: 'Will this provide structuring opportunities?'. This is code for: 'Do we need to put in anti-abuse provisions?'. A related piece of code is the term: 'management intent'. The members of the Board generally do not like leaving something open to the entity to choose which way it accounts for something depending on what it plans to do with it. IAS 39 requires management to specify what they plan to do with financial assets, but they then cannot change their view subsequently. The rule that you cannot change your mind is an anti-abuse rule, aimed at stopping you selecting which gains you recognize now and which you defer. Recently the vocabulary has changed, and management intent is becoming 'business model'.

This is an ongoing confrontation between different Board members and also between outside regulators. To generalize, one could say that Europeans do not push the limits of standards the way the Americans do, and consequently they do not understand or appreciate anti-abuse rules. They think that the standards should help you show the business as it is – to reflect the business model. As some point out, the business model is something that can be observed over a period, whereas management intent is intangible and can change instantly. As the founder members of the Board have left, sentiment in the IASB has probably changed on this. Pressure from outside has helped. IFRS 9 *Financial Instruments*, the replacement for IAS 39, does indeed ask people to classify financial assets according to their business model, and allows them to change classification if the model changes.

There is more reluctance in the US. During the debate on lessor accounting there were two competing accounting approaches to lessor accounting. In joint discussion with the FASB the Boards came to the conclusion that one approach was more relevant to an entity whose business was renting equipment (such as a car hire, or plant hire business) and an entity whose business was providing finance (such as aircraft leasing). The IASB said that was fine, they would just tell people to decide which business model they had and apply the accounting that went with that. The FASB refused, saying that would not work in their environment. They needed rules to enable people to know which side of the line they fell. So the exposure draft now includes guidelines as to what package of services is offered to determine whether it is rental or financing, to avoid leaving any management choice.

> **Board members are becoming more pragmatic and less impressed with accounting models as such**

I would observe that much of the above refers to the period since April 2001 when the IASB had its first public meeting. I believe that this period was dominated by experienced standard-setters who were influenced by the inflationary period in the 1970s and the need to converge with the US. I think the consensus within the Board is changing as the composition changes. Board members are becoming more pragmatic and less impressed with accounting models as such. I would cite the abandonment of 'own credit risk' as an example. In IFRS 9 the IASB decided that while fair value includes reflecting own credit risk in the measurement of liabilities, it would not mandate this as it produced results that were counter-intuitive. As one standard-setter put it: it failed the 'does it make sense?' test.

Conclusions

This is a chapter largely of personal observation; some backed up by research but much of it subjective judgement based on continuing observation. I have pointed out that the IASB is a committee, and makes decisions by majority vote; consequently it may be inconsistent overall because of the diversity of views within that committee. The members of the committee also change, which impacts where the majority lies. I have suggested that the trend in Board appointments is away from standard-setters and towards regulators, and towards involving a smaller proportion of English mother tongue members.

In relation to the ideas that inform their standard-setting I have pointed out that they are obliged to be guided by the Conceptual Framework, and this has led in the first decade to a stance where they look at changes in assets and liabilities as the fundamental building blocks of performance measurement. This may make them more susceptible to recognizing executory contracts and moving the boundaries of recognition. I note that anti-abuse issues are given a good deal of prominence, and much of this derives from US experience.

FURTHER READING

Aisbitt, S. (2006) 'Assessing the effect of the transition of IFRS on equity: the case of the FTSE 100' *Accounting in Europe*, 3: 117–134.

André, P., Cazavan-Jeny, A., Dick, W., Richard, C. & Walton, P. (2009) "Fair value accounting and the banking crisis in 2008: shooting the messenger' *Accounting in Europe*, 6: 3–24.

Barth, M., Clinch, G. & Shibano, T. (1999) 'International accounting harmonization and global equity markets' *Journal of Accounting and Economics*, 26: 201–235.

Bay, W. & Bruns, H-G. (2003) 'Multinational companies and international capital markets' in Walton, P., Haller, A. & Raffournier, B. *International Accounting* 2nd ed, Thomson Learning, London: 385–403.

Benston, G., Bromwich, M., Litan, R.E. & Wagenhofer, A. (2006) *Worldwide Financial Reporting: The Development and Future of Accounting Standards*, Oxford University Press, Oxford.

Bocqueraz, C. & Walton, P. (2006) 'Creating a supranational institution: the role of the individual and the mood of the times' *Accounting History*, 11: 271–288.

Bradbury, M. (2007) 'An anatomy of an IFRIC Interpretation' *Accounting in Europe*, 4: 109–122.

Cairns, D. (2006) 'The use of fair value in IFRS' *Accounting in Europe*, 3: 5–22.

Camfferman, K. & Zeff, S. (2007) *Financial Reporting and Global Capital Markets: A History of the International Accounting Standards Committee, 1973–2000*, Oxford University Press, Oxford.

Cooper, S. (2007) 'Performance measurement for equity analysis and valuation' *Accounting in Europe*, 4: 1–50.

Dao, T.H.P. (2005) 'Monitoring compliance with IFRS: some insights from the French regulatory system' *Accounting in Europe*, 2: 107–136.

Daske, H. (2006) 'Economic benefits of adopting IFRS or US-GAAP – have the expected costs of equity capital really decreased?' *Journal of Business Finance and Accounting*, 33: 329–373.

Delvaille, P., Ebbers, G. & Saccon, C. (2005) 'International financial reporting convergence: evidence from three continental European countries' *Accounting in Europe*, 2: 137–164.

Dick, W. & Walton, P. (2007) 'The Agenda of the IASB: a moving target' *Australian Accounting Review*, August.

Erchinger, H. & Melcher, W. (2007) 'Convergence between US GAAP and IFRS: acceptance of IFRS by the US Securities and Exchange Commission' *Accounting in Europe*, 4: 123–140.

Gélard, G. (2004) 'What can be expected from accounting standards?' *Accounting in Europe*, 1: 17–20.

Hague, I.P. (2004) 'IAS 39: underlying principles' *Accounting in Europe*, 1: 21–26.

Haller, A. (2003) 'Segmental reporting' in Walton, P., Haller, A. & Raffournier, B. *International Accounting* 2nd ed, Thomson Learning, London: 444–470.

Johnson, L.T. & Petrone, K.R. (1998) 'Is goodwill an asset?' *Accounting Horizons*, September.

Lamb, M. (1995) 'When is a group a group? Convergence of concepts of "group" in European Union corporation tax' *European Accounting Review*, 4(1).

Larson, K. (2007) 'Constituent participation and the IASB's International Financial Reporting Interpretations Committee' *Accounting in Europe*, 4: 207–254.

Nobes, C.W. (2006) 'The survival of international differences under IFRS: towards a research agenda' *Accounting and Business Research*, 36(3).

Richard, J. (2004) 'The secret past of fair value: lessons from history applied to the French case' *Accounting in Europe*, 1: 95–108.

Schipper, K. (2005) 'The introduction of International Accounting Standards in Europe: implications for international convergence' *European Accounting Review*, 14: 101–126.

Soderstrom, N. & Sun, K.J. (2007) 'IFRS adoption and accounting quality' *European Accounting Review*, 16: 675–702.

Taylor, P.A (2003) 'Foreign currency translation' in Walton, P., Haller, A. & Raffournier, B. *International Accounting* 2nd ed, Thomson Learning, London: 405–442.

Tokar, M. (2005) 'Convergence and the implementation of a single set of global standards: the real life challenge' *Accounting in Europe*, 2: 47–68.

UNCTAD Secretariat (2003) 'Accounting needs of developing countries' in Walton, P., Haller, A. & Raffournier, B. *International Accounting* 2nd ed. Thomson Learning, London: 366–384.

Van Mourik, C. (2010) 'The equity theories and financial reporting: an analysis' *Accounting in Europe*, 7: 191–211.

Walton, P. (1993) 'The true and fair view in British accounting' *European Accounting Review*, 2: 49–58.

Walton, P. (1998) 'Benson's projects take a decisive turn' *Accountancy and Finance Update* (South Africa) 3: 7/9.

Walton, P. (1998) 'Henry Benson' in Warner, M. (ed) *The IEBM Handbook of Management Thinking*, International Thomson Publishing, London: 482–486.

Walton, P. (2003) 'European harmonisation' in Choi, F.D.S. (ed) *International Accounting and Finance Handbook* 2nd ed, John Wiley & Sons, New York: 17.1–17.17.

Walton, P. (2004) 'IAS 39: where different accounting models collide' *Accounting in Europe*, 1: 5–16.

Walton, P. (2006) 'Fair value and executory contracts: moving the boundaries in international financial reporting' *Accounting and Business Research*, 36: 337–343.

Walton, P. (ed) (2007) *The Routledge Guide to Fair Value and Financial Reporting*, Routledge, Abingdon.

Whittington, G. (2005) 'The adoption of International Accounting Standards in the European Union' *European Accounting Review*, 14: 127–153.

Wüstemann, J. & Kierzek, S. (2005) 'Revenue recognition under IFRS revisited: conceptual models, current proposals and practical consequences' *Accounting in Europe*, 2: 69–106.

INDEX